The Belt Cookie Table Cookbook

Happy Baking!

— bonnie tau

The Belt Cookie Table Cookbook

Bonnie Tawse

Belt Publishing

Printed in the United States of America
First edition 2020
2 3 4 5 6 7 8 9

ISBN: 978-1-948742-83-2

Belt Publishing
3143 W. 33rd Street #6
Cleveland, Ohio 44109
www.beltpublishing.com

Cover by David Wilson
Book design by Meredith Pangrace

Table of Contents

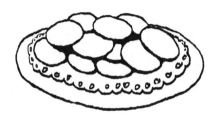

FOREWORD

O f course this cookbook contains a recipe for clothespin cookies, flaky pastry cylinders filled with sweet cream and a fixture of the Youngstown, Ohio, cookie table. A little over an hour's drive away, across the Pennsylvania border, in my hometown of Pittsburgh and the surrounding counties—what you might call the eastern end of the cookie-table belt—we know these as lady locks and we, too, dutifully include them on most every cookie table. I say "we," but that's presumptuous. My heritage is German and Irish; I grew up Roman Catholic. A descendant of the Mennonites who settled in Pennsylvania beginning in the seventeenth century would likely call these cream horns. The most important thing to know about them is that they're delicious.

The most important thing to know about this book is that it's full of recipes for delicious cookies. And you can make them—which is not to say they're all easy. This isn't one of those cookbooks promising quick, no-brainer recipes for the overextended twenty-first-century person looking to destress on the weekend. These are recipes with resonance. They measure out a whole world by the teaspoon and cupful.

Maybe you're not a baker. Maybe you've picked up this book out of historical or ethnographic curiosity, planning to read the headnotes at the top of each recipe for context and skip the recipes themselves. You'd learn plenty that way: Bonnie Tawse does an impressive job, beginning in her introduction, of situating the cookie table in a place, Northeast Ohio, and time, the twentieth-century industrial boom that brought immigrants there from Italy, Ireland, Poland, Greece, and too many other places to list here, carrying their cookie recipes with them. Not a native of Youngstown herself, she's able to describe, vividly, the experience of encountering her very first cookie table, its giddy abundance—

some 8,000 cookies!—and the strategy involved in assembling a satisfactory plateful. Those recipe headnotes bring us the voices of the bakers who contributed their beloved cookies, each one a snapshot of a family, its history and habits and place in a larger community. You can hear the Del Sinchak Polka Band playing, see the bride twirling on the dance floor with dollars pinned to her dress.

But please, don't skip the recipes. Study the ingredient lists. Does the abundance of Crisco called for surprise you? Consider what it means. In her book *American Cookie*, Anne Byrn talks about how loaded with information a single ingredient can be. A rural cook would have had plenty of lard to use, while for a city dweller in the early twentieth century, Crisco, a recent invention, would have been more accessible. And any baker who knew what she was doing would have been delighted by the shortening's high melting point, key to producing tender pastry.

Just look at how it's used in that recipe for clothespin cookies, contributed by Brad and Marjorie Gessner, who begin by discussing the merits of the disposable pastry bags they have today versus the aluminum frosting tube with a plunger they used, growing up, to fill the dainty confections with cream. The daintiness of the cookie can be attributed largely to a process called laminating, in which the dough is spread with shortening and then folded, again and again, producing flaky layers. It's the same process used to make croissants and a whole range of Viennese pastries, of which clothespins are, after all, a cousin. As you read, visualize the process, step by step. You're young Marjorie Gessner at the elbow of her mother, a little awed at the metamorphosis of ordinary flour and Crisco into something so elegant. You'd be proud, perhaps even a bit smug, to plant a platter of these on the cookie table at a neighbor's wedding, a testament to your family's traditions and shared appreciation for a thing done well.

Take a step further and make the cookies, and you're traveling through time in a very tactile way: building a bridge to the past or a particular culture by reenacting its rituals and crafts. Recipes are miraculous documents. So many histories fail to do justice to the everyday labor that puts food on the table and knits a neighborhood together. Through the recipes in this book you can inhabit several dozen different kitchens. You can travel through time in a very tactile way. I don't mean to suggest that the cookies collected here are mere relics. One of the great things about cookies is how adaptable they are. Read on to learn about the innovations different generations have brought to their family recipes. The cookie table is very much a living tradition. It continues to evolve. Taste it for yourself.

Beth Kracklauer
Pittsburgh, May 2020

INTRODUCTION

C ookie tables: what's not to love about a tradition that goes back to the turn of the century, when wedding cakes were far too dear for newly arrived immigrants to purchase? When family and friends showed their affection and support to a bride and groom by baking from scratch hundreds (sometimes thousands) of cookies and other small sweet treats to be shared with guests at the reception? A tradition that has built into it the idea that not only should you eat as many cookies as you possibly can at the celebration, but also encourages you to take some home with you—and toward which end the hosts leave small bags or boxes so you can do just that? For a city that has far too often been defined by industrial decay or seemingly unstoppable corruption, the cookie table tradition of Youngstown, Pittsburgh, and parts in between provides a welcome and authentic counter-narrative and an unwavering source of local pride—no matter what side of town you grew up on.

And really, what's not to love about cookies? Cookies from different cultures, cookies with different textures, spices, shapes, and backstories. Simple cookies, ridiculously indulgent cookies. Cookies that aren't really cookies at all but slices of yeasted breads, or more like candy, but are lumped into the cookie category because they are delicious and someone's great-grandmother brought the recipe with her when she came over from the old country? When I was asked by Belt Publishing if I would consider editing a cookbook about the cookie table tradition, I said "yes" without hesitation.

There was just one catch: while I have a lifelong love of baking, and of cookies in particular, I had actually never been to a Youngstown wedding or experienced a cookie table in person.

I was ready to tell my Martha Bayne, my editor, that she should probably find someone else for the job when I stumbled across an announcement for an event in February of 2020: the Cookie Table and Cocktail Gala, hosted by the Mahoning Valley Historical Society. It was going to take place in just a few weeks and there were still a handful of tickets left. This was my chance! The announcement said that there would be thousands of cookies, most of them made and donated by home bakers. It also said there would be a polka band. So I bought a ticket, booked a room at an Airbnb, and told my husband and children that I would be gone for a couple of days.

"What exactly are you going to be doing?" asked my husband.

I said, barely able to hold back a smile, "Cookie table research."

And so, on a cold and rainy winter Saturday, I got in my Honda CRV and left Chicago, barrelling down I-80 headed for Youngstown. I made a quick stop in Toledo for a gas and a chili dog from Tony Packo's and at about 6:30 p.m. I drove up to the at-capacity parking lot of the Our Lady of Mount Carmel Basilica, where masses of people were making their way towards the entrance of the social hall for the eighth annual Cookie Table and Cocktails event.

The hall was decorated with a gambling theme and packed with people milling around large banquet tables. There was a bar in the back, bustling; the stage all set for the Del Sinchak Polka Band. A large buffet already had a line forming—an Italian spread from a local caterer. And then I spotted it. Tucked into a back alcove was the cookie table. It was massive, laid out in a U-shape. The cookies were elegantly displayed on platters and tiered towers at varying heights. The seemingly endless buffet offered up an estimated 8,000 cookies, baked and donated by about eighty-five different people, the bulk of them amateur home bakers. And, much to my surprise, the table, with its incredible array of cookies in different shapes and colors, was being guarded by several members of Youngstown State University's football team, specifically, its defensive line. Apparently this detail was now necessary to keep people from rushing the cookie table before it was time and sampling the baked goods too soon. This cookie table was the real deal, so much so that it needed its own security.

I waited until it was my table's turn, and with the strategic help of a few of new friends from Table #43, I approached the cookie table with the awe of a small child combined with the scanning eye of a researcher. Pretty much every classic cookie table cookie was present: Clothespins, Kolachi, Nut Kiffles, Pecan Tassies, and more. But there were also many that were new to me: Coconut Islands, a riff on the Buckeye in the shape of Ohio, a fried Italian morsel called an Uandi.

You get to choose just thirteen cookies for your plate. People take their selections seriously because the offerings are so vast, but you also have to keep the line moving. And should you try to add one more, you will be gently but firmly admonished by a hulking twenty-something in a red YSU jersey. In the spirit of a cookie table at an actual wedding, once everyone has had a chance to fill their plate, you have the option to also fill a small box with cookies to take home. You bet that I went back and filled my box just to the top (those are the rules, no over-stuffing) with the cookies that I hadn't yet tried, as well as those that I had and liked very much. I had made a pilgrimage of sorts to Youngstown in the name of the cookie table tradition. I was not going home empty handed.

Back at my Airbnb, hopped up on sugar, my box of cookies locked in my car, I realized that I had just been part of a powerful moment of pride, tradition, memory, and community—all in the context of cookies. I also realized that I needed to get to it and start collecting recipes.

In the ensuing weeks I received recipes from people I met at the event, people I reached out to on the Youngstown Cookie Table Facebook group (yes, that's a thing and it has 15,000 members all over the world), writers who had published pieces in Belt's 2015 Youngstown anthology, *Car Bombs to Cookie Tables* (the 2020 second edition of which inspired this complementary book), people I have known for decades but never knew they had roots in the Youngstown area, and mothers-in-law of friends. The recipes came handwritten, as screenshots, scans of index cards, pictures of stained sections of cookbooks, and neatly typed Word documents. Several came from home cookbooks already put together to chronicle family recipes. Many of them had been translated from another language or had to be walked through over the phone to make sure the quantities and the steps were just right. Several were written in an incredible shorthand that assumes that everyone knows how to bake not only cookies but pies, tarts, pastry crust, and yeasted doughs.

The recipes were tested in my own home kitchen (a few friends helped with several of the trickier ones) and most of the recipe testing took place during the first months of the COVID-19 crisis, with Illinois's stay-at-home order in place. If going to the Cookie Table and Cocktails event was a sweet research gig (and my last public event before the shutdown), being at home covered in flour, with hands shiny with butter or Crisco, was a beautiful distraction and meaningful task during the uncertainty of the unfolding pandemic. I also got to learn many times over the simple but sweet rewards of gifting home-baked goods.

Though I did not have a proper cookie table at a wedding or graduation celebration to contribute to (and, sadly, no one at the time of this writing probably will) I was able to gift my "test cookies" to my suddenly unemployed neighbors across the hall, and to my friends a few buildings down the way, one of whom is immuno-compromised and pretty much stuck at home.

Roseli de Silva's Brazalian Brigadeiros and Carol Brungardt Mound's Pecan Petites ended up going to the mental health unit where my neighbor Amy works, the cookies acting as a sweet salve to an exhausted group of therapists and nurses. Grandma McKnight's Sugar Cookies and Grace Murray's Grandmother Margaret's Molasses Cookies ended up getting packed into the free lunches given to clients at Chicago's suddenly overwhelmed Common Pantry food pantry. My neighbor Guy, an out-of-work actor, still sings the praises of Margaret Trickett-Healey's Pecan Pie Bars. I think he is legitimately crestfallen that my cookie testing phase has ended.

I have come to realize that a huge part of the cookie table tradition is the gift of time and intention. So when someone bakes eight dozen Pizzelles or hand-dips twelve dozen Buckeyes, whether you eat them at a wedding, at a college graduation gathering, or a special event like the Cookie Table and Cocktails gala, remember that that baker gathered the ingredients and spent several hours (or days) in their kitchen with the sole intention of bringing you and your circle of family and friends a little, delicious moment of joy. You have been given the edible gift of someone's time.

The cookie table is also a way to have someone present who cannot be there physically. It keeps memories alive. This truth was repeated multiple times by the people who submitted recipes to this book: "My mother wasn't able to be at the wedding but by having her cookies there, she was there in spirit." Someone's favorite cookie recipe provides a connection to specific moments in the past. For Alec Ring, it is his Polish grandfather dunking his Croatian Kifli cookies into his cup of coffee. If the recipe comes from Wales, or Brazil, or your grandma's kitchen on Austin Ave., when you serve that cookie, you have played a part in making sure the history is still very much alive in the world, one sweet bite at a time.

The people in Youngstown and Pittsburgh and all points in between are proud of this tradition, they make sure to keep it going. It is a point of civic, familial, and cultural pride. That said, it is not so rigid that it isn't up for interpretation or modernization. For example, the two young men who were my hosts at my Airbnb made sure that I knew they were going to have a cookie table at their wedding in May in Pittsburgh. New cookies such as neon-colored Macarons and shortbread infused with floral notes of lavender or Earl Grey tea are both welcome and then riffed upon. People who move away from the eastern Ohio or Pittsburgh area often still have cookie tables as part of their celebrations, to make sure that people know where they come from and that this tradition is important to them.

At its core, the cookie table is a simple but meaningful way for people to show their affection, by way of baking dozens (or hundreds) of cookies, no matter the occasion. As contributor Anna Pitinii Hood puts it, "Family, love, cookies—they are synonymous." I hope that this cookbook helps you tap into some of that connection.

A Note on Assumptions of Knowledge and Skills

A strong cookie tradition does not persist in an entire region for more than a hundred years if the people who come from that place aren't solid in the skills of baking. Most of the people who submitted recipes for this cookbook said that they were taught how to bake by their mothers or grandmothers and many shared recipes from generations before them. When recipes are handed down generation after generation, by people who know how to bake and are sharing recipes with others who also know how to bake, a certain shorthand begins to evolve. The assumption is that the person receiving the recipe already has a basic foundation of kitchen knowledge.

This became abundantly clear with the first recipe I received. It said to "combine the flour, butter, and brown sugar until a pie dough consistency is formed." If you bake pies all the time, then this would be no problem and you would just keep rolling through the recipe. But what if you have never made pie dough before? What if you've made a pie but you've always bought a pre-made pie crust from the grocery store? Then you would probably not know that the butter should be cold and cut up into smaller pieces. That you should work the butter into the flour and brown sugar, either with a pastry cutter or two knives or by simply using your fingers? That the consistency you are working towards is first going to be moist and crumbly, but that then the butter and flour and sugar will bind together and the dough will slowly form?

In gathering and testing these recipes, I and my helpful test bakers were moved (and sometimes humbled) by how much most of the bakers assumed the average person already knows. We appreciate brevity, especially when walking through steps on longer recipes, but in editing these recipes we did our best to break down instructions in a manner that is helpful to everyone—especially those of us who still have emerging baking skills. A lovely example of someone handing down her own practical kitchen wisdom and assuming in the best way possible that we pretty much know what we need to do is in Marie McNulty's mother Yola's recipe for Chocolate Cookies. It's a massive recipe, unapologetically geared toward baking for a large crowd. After telling you to "add flour gradually until a stiff dough is formed"— this is five pounds of flour, mind you—she adds, "Use your best judgment." And so we pass that directive over to you.

Multiple voices came together to create this book; to distinguish those of the contributors from that of the author, introductory recipe text is set in italics when the individual contributor is speaking in the first person.

RECIPES

Apricot Cookies

Delores Rembowski and Carissa Benchwick

This cookie recipe was a favorite of my mother, Delores Rembowski. She grew up in the country close to Shillings Mill Berlin Center, Ohio. Her maiden name was Delores Teeters. She grew up during the Depression, helping out with her five brothers. Both of her parents worked, so my mother learned to cook and bake at a very young age. She married my father, Stephan Rembowski, in the early 50s and moved to the west side of Youngstown. My father came from a family of ten boys and one girl. His father was an immigrant from Poland. Living on the west side was a mixture of numerous different nationalities. The elder females in the neighborhood would spend time with the younger women and give cooking lessons. The babcia (Polish), nonna (Italian), oma (German), yia yia (Greek)— all the grandmas! They all came. Such a great memory. Sadly, my mother passed away from cancer in 2013. My daughter (Delores's granddaughter) is the only one in the family that can bake these cookies like my mom did. In fact, Carissa entered these cookies in the 2018 Youngstown Cookie Table and Cocktails event and was awarded Top Baker, Judges Choice. It was such a night! My daughter and mother were both honored in such a sweet way.

INGREDIENTS

1 cup Crisco
8 ounces cream cheese, softened
2 egg yolks
2 cups flour
1 jar apricot filling (Baker is the family's preferred brand, or see following recipe for homemade lekvar filling)
or
nut filling (below)
powdered sugar (for dusting)

PREPARATION

In a large bowl, mix the Crisco and cream cheese. Add the egg yolks one at a time and stir to combine. Slowly mix in the flour and scrape the sides of the bowl until it all comes together in a soft dough. Form into a ball and wrap in plastic wrap. Put wrapped dough in the refrigerator for two hours or overnight. This is a very soft dough, so it is easiest to work with when it is cold.

Preheat the oven to 350 degrees F. Remove dough from the refrigerator and cut into four equal parts. Return three of the parts of dough to the refrigerator, to keep chilled.

One part at a time, roll dough out on a powdered-sugared surface, using a lightly floured rolling pin. Roll dough to a roughly 8 x 8 inches square, about ⅛ of an inch thick. Using a pizza cutter or very sharp knife. cut dough into 2-inch squares and transfer to an ungreased cookie sheet. Fill each square with one scant teaspoon of apricot or nut filling. With that same square, take the left corner of the dough and bring it to the center, gently pressing into the middle of the filling. Take the edge of the right corner and bring it to the middle, pressing it on top of the other corner. Your cookies should have a diamond shape with the two corners coming together in the center.

Bake for approximately 10–12 minutes until lightly browned. Cool on racks and once cool, dust with powdered sugar.

NUT FILLING

1 ½ cups ground nuts such as walnuts or pecans
½ teaspoon vanilla

Mix together with enough sugar to taste and milk to moisten.

Makes about 60 cookies. Delores's note on the recipe card said she usually doubled it.

Apricot Filling (Lekvar)

Bonnie Tawse

Many of the home bakers who submitted recipes to this cookbook listed a favorite commercial fruit filling for making Kiffle, Cornuletes, or Kolache, especially when making them in large quantities for a cookie table. But should you have dried apricots on hand, this recipe has excellent flavor and it will not run when baked. Lekvar is a traditional Central and Eastern European fruit filling made with fresh plums or apricots, or with dried fruit such as prunes and, here, dried apricots. This filling is excellent in Delores Rembowski's Apricot Cookies.

INGREDIENTS

2 cups dried, pitted apricots
1 cup water
¼ cup orange juice
½ cup sugar
2 tablespoons lemon juice
pinch salt

PREPARATION

Put all of the ingredients in a saucepan, stir, and bring to a boil for one minute.

Reduce heat to low, so that it's at a steady simmer, cover pan, and simmer for 30 minutes.

Remove lid from pan. Let apricots simmer an additional 2–4 minutes, stirring frequently until most of the liquid has been absorbed or evaporated. There should be about 3 tablespoons of liquid left in the pan.

Remove pan from heat and mash the apricots using a potato masher until a smooth puree forms. You can drag a fork through the mixture to catch any large pieces of apricot and simply mash those again.

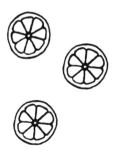

Betty's Baklava

Anna Pitinii Hood

If you know any Greek people, you know that they are serious about food. My parents, Betty and Mike Pitinii, had another reason: a household of ten! My family is from Niles, Ohio, where my parents, grandmother, five sisters, and one brother all lived together. Celebrations were important! At Christmas, aunts, uncles, and cousins all came to our house. Everyone brought Greek delights. Looking back, my mother and aunts each had their specialties, which were passed down in the family. When the weddings started rolling around, the cookie planning started! Each of my sisters have their specialties—Baklava, Kourabiedes, Finikia—and cousins and aunts contributed theirs as well. Getting together the morning of a family member's wedding was the start to a celebration of love. We needed carts to get all those cookies into the kitchen coolers at the hall! Now, my sisters and I are planning the cookies for our own children's weddings. Family, love, cookies—they are synonymous.

INGREDIENTS
SYRUP

3 cups white sugar
1½ cups water
2 tablespoons freshly squeezed lemon juice
1 cinnamon stick
½ cup honey

In a medium saucepan combine sugar, water, lemon juice, and cinnamon stick. Set pan over medium heat and stir until sugar dissolves. Bring to a boil, stirring every few minutes for a total of 10 minutes. Slowly add the honey, bring to a boil again, stirring constantly. Boil 5 more minutes. Remove from heat and let cool.

Discard the cinnamon stick.

BAKLAVA PASTRY

1 pound filo dough, thawed (if using frozen) and cut to fit a
9 x 13-inch pan; keep it covered with a lightly damp but NOT
wet thin cloth
1 pound melted butter
1 pound coarsely ground walnuts
½ cup sugar
1 teaspoon ground cinnamon
½ teaspoon ground nutmeg
whole cloves

PREPARATION

In a large mixing bowl combine walnuts, sugar, cinnamon, and
nutmeg. Set aside. Place your ingredients and tools close to the
pan: cut filo covered with a light damp cloth, walnut blend,
melted butter, and pastry brush. Brush the bottom of the pan
with butter. One at a time, place 12 layers of filo in the pan,
brushing each layer of filo with butter. Sprinkle ½ cup walnuts
evenly over the 12 layers of buttered filo. Add 3 more layers of
filo, buttering each. Sprinkle another ½ cup of the nuts, and
butter three more layers of filo, repeat these steps until all nuts
are used up, making sure to reserve 12 layers of filo. Layer these
final 12 sheets of filo on top, buttering each. Put the pan in the
refrigerator for at least half an hour. The pastry is too fragile to cut
unless the butter hardens.

Preheat the oven to 400 degrees F.

Before putting pastry in the oven, cut it into diamond shapes
using a very sharp knife and the following technique: Cut a

¼-inch slice down each side of the long sides of the pan. This will give you more perfect pieces without the edge ruffle. With a thin plastic ruler (that has been washed), cut 8 long columns. Angle the ruler and begin cutting diamond shaped pieces starting at one corner of the pan and cutting the other corner on the opposite end. Repeat until all the diamond shapes are cut. Some will be slightly smaller than others. Put 1 whole clove in each piece, even pieces that are not full diamonds.

Make sure the oven is at 400 degrees before putting baklava in. Bake for 15 minutes, then reduce the oven to 350 degrees. Continue baking for 45-50 minutes until the pastry is golden brown.

Remove pastry from oven and gently spoon cooled syrup evenly over pastry. This recipe yields a healthy amount of syrup, so you might have more than you need. Err on the side of being generous with it but you might have some left over.

Let baklava sit uncovered in a cool place for at least 24 hours before removing pieces.

To serve, put each piece of baklava in a small muffin cup.

Makes about 75 baklava pieces.

Biscotti

Ange and Vince Guerrieri

This recipe is from my grandmother, Ange Guerrieri. My wife Shannon makes a ton of cookies every Christmas—among my presents for her previously were a pizzelle iron for her birthday and a KitchenAid mixer for Christmas, which I gave her early so she could make cookies with it—and most of them are from her own family recipes. But this (my grandmother's recipe) is the recipe she uses for biscotti.

INGREDIENTS

2 cups toasted sliced almonds
6 eggs
3 ½ cups flour
1 ½ cup sugar
1 cup vegetable oil
4 teaspoons baking powder
2 tablespoons vanilla

PREPARATION

Preheat the oven to 350 degrees F.

Beat eggs, adding sugar gradually, until smooth. Add oil and vanilla. Sift flour and baking powder and add it to egg mixture; mix gently until all flour is incorporated. Mix in almonds and shape into long, flat loaves about 2 inches wide and half an inch tall. Place on a floured cookie sheet and bake for about 10 minutes.

Remove from the oven, transfer to a cooling rack, and allow to cool for 5 minutes. Slice pieces about half an inch thick. Put slices on their sides back on the cookie sheet and return to the oven and toast until golden brown.

Brigadeiros: Traditional Brazilian Chocolate Truffles

Roseli da Silva

When Anna Hood's son married the daughter of Roseli da Silva, the two mothers came together to make sure there was a proper cookie table at the couple's reception in Youngstown. Anna's family is from Ohio, so didn't have too far to travel, but the bride's family is from Brazil. That did not stop her mother, sisters, and aunties from traveling to the states and joining in on the baking and preparations. These truffles were served on the cookie table (along with Anna's mother's baklava) and are a perfect recipe for an assembly line of helpers.

INGREDIENTS

1 14-ounce can sweetened condensed milk
¼ cup 100% cocoa powder
1 tablespoon unsalted butter
1 pinch of salt
½ cup chocolate sprinkles

PREPARATION

In a heavy bottomed pot on medium heat, add the sweetened condensed milk and whisk in the cocoa powder until combined. Add the butter and salt and stir continuously for about 10 minutes (do not burn). The mixture is complete when you can tilt the pan and see the bottom of the pot for 2–3 seconds when dragging a spatula through it.

Carefully pour into a greased pan, cover with plastic wrap, and chill in the fridge for 3 hours or overnight.

Scoop the mixture—which will now be quite dense—into greased hands (butter is traditional) and roll into 1-inch balls. (This step is great to do with a team.)

Toss the balls in a large mixing bowl with chocolate sprinkles to coat, and finish by rolling in your hands to press the sprinkles into place. Serve each in a small pastry cup.

Note: Do not roll the fudge balls with buttered hands and then immediately try to roll them in the chocolate sprinkles. This will just make the sprinkles greasy and then it will be even harder to get them to stick. Keep the two steps separate.

This recipe makes about 20 brigadeiros.

Buckeyes

Kelly Kress and Mary Stano Musick

This is a cookie recipe used by my grandmother, Mary Stano Musick. My mom's family is from Slovakia, my grandmother was the first generation to be born in the U.S. My grandparents settled in Warren and my mom grew up there; my parents live in Florida now but I still have a lot of family in eastern Ohio. This is a recipe from a cookbook my mom, Maryann Musick Kress, made for all the grandchildren. I remember helping my mom make the buckeyes when I was a child, they were always my favorite.

INGREDIENTS

1 cup smooth peanut butter
¼ cup butter, softened
1 teaspoon vanilla
1 ½ cups powdered sugar
1 12-ounce bag of semi-sweet chocolate chips
1 bar of paraffin or 1 tablespoon shortening

PREPARATION

Cream together peanut butter and butter. Mix in vanilla and powdered sugar. Shape dough into 1-inch balls; if dough doesn't have a smooth appearance once rolled, you can wet your hands with a bit of water. Place on a tray covered with wax paper. Insert a toothpick into each ball. Place in the freezer to chill until very firm, at least 30 minutes.

Melt the chocolate chips and the shortening or paraffin in a double boiler or in a bowl in the microwave, times will vary for different ovens.

Remove peanut butter balls from the freezer. Dip each ball into the melted chocolate, leaving the top "undipped" so a small circle of peanut butter is still visible. Place back on the wax-paper-covered tray. You might have to reheat the chocolate if it starts to cool and stiffen as you are coating the peanut butter balls. Remove toothpicks and, using your finger, smooth over the toothpick hole. Put the tray in the refrigerator until the chocolate is chilled and set.

Cardamom Meringues

Benjamin Morgan

This recipe is a twist on a traditional French meringue that I was inspired to make for my first Cookie Table and Cocktails competition. The mixture of spices came from a lot of trial and error coupled with plenty of "guinea pig" testing on family, friends, and schoolmates. Along with the ingredients listed below, these cookies are best made alongside the people you love and, even though this recipe is brand new, it has already given us many warm memories. An additional trick to keep in mind: meringues do best in warm, dry weather, but won't suffer much in rainy weather as long as they are well ventilated and promptly eaten.

INGREDIENTS

3 egg whites
1 cup superfine sugar
1/8 teaspoon cream of tartar
1 teaspoon vanilla
1/2 teaspoon and a pinch cardamom
1/4 teaspoon ground ginger
1/4 teaspoon ground cinnamon
1/8 teaspoon chili powder

PREPARATION

Preheat the oven to 215 degrees F. Separate eggs, being very careful not to get any yolk into the egg whites. Beat egg whites on high until they foam, and continue to mix as you add the cream of tartar and vanilla. Add in the spices as the mixture becomes stiffer, then begin adding the sugar, one teaspoon at a time, until the egg whites start to form soft peaks. Continue to mix until stiff peaks are formed, making sure not to overmix. Once the mixture is the correct consistency, either pipe or spoon* disks 1–1 ½ inches in diameter onto cookie sheets lined with parchment paper, making sure to leave room for expansion. Bake for 1 ½ hours, checking to make sure that the meringues are light, airy, and fully dry all the way through. Allow to cool for 20 minutes.

*Be careful not to knock the bowl or shake the meringue too much. Doing so will ultimately make them denser.

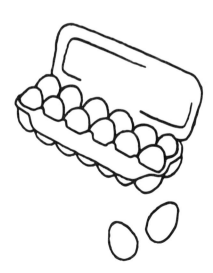

Cherry Coconut Bars

Marilyn Rohrbaugh

This recipe is from Judy Rohrbaugh's mother-in-law Marilyn, who grew up in Youngstown but now lives in Ft. Meyers, Florida. Judy says that she made these for many special occasions and that everyone loved them. The combination of butter, nuts, cherries, and coconut make for a rich and ever so slightly gooey treat. (But not too gooey for a cookie table!) When testing this recipe, we could not get Maraschino cherries, but we did find sour cherries in syrup. They worked just fine and actually dialed the sweetness back—so either will work here, choose whatever cherry makes you happy!

INGREDIENTS
BASE

½ cup flour
¼ teaspoon baking soda
½ cup packed brown sugar
½ cup rolled oats (not quick cooking)
⅓ cup butter or margarine, melted

TOPPING

¼ cup flour
¾ cup sugar
½ teaspoon baking powder
2 eggs, beaten
¾ cup Maraschino or sour cherries, cut up in quarters
½ cup flaked sweetened coconut
½ cup chopped nuts

Preparation

Preheat the oven to 350 degrees F.

In a bowl, mix all the ingredients for the base layer. Press evenly into an 8 x 8-inch square pan.

In another bowl, combine all topping ingredients. Mix well. Spread on top of base layer. Bake for 30 minutes. Allow to cool thoroughly before cutting into small squares.

Makes 12 squares. Recipe can be doubled for a 9 x 13-inch pan.

Chocolate Cherry Candy

Rita Pitoscia

While the Youngstown cookie table tradition is mostly about a table teeming with baked goods, it can often include someone bringing their version of a homemade truffle or other handmade candy. Rita Pitoscia's daughter Judy Rohrbaugh said that this recipe was one her mother's favorites and she was known for making these for everyone's wedding. She also added that her sister could eat the whole batch!

INGREDIENTS

1 cup semi-sweet chocolate chips or pieces (8 ounces)
⅓ cup evaporated milk (Rita preferred the PET brand)
1 ½ cup powdered sugar
⅓ cup nuts, chopped fine (walnuts, almonds, or pecans)
⅓ cup Maraschino cherries, well drained and chopped
1 ¼ cup fine shredded sweetened coconut

PREPARATION

In a heavy 2-quart saucepan, stir chocolate chips or pieces and evaporated milk over very low heat until the chocolate melts and both are blended. Remove from heat. Stir in powdered sugar, chopped nuts and Maraschino cherry pieces until well mixed. Chill until mixture is cool enough to handle.

Using a teaspoon, scoop out mixture and then roll by hand into balls, then roll in the shredded coconut to coat the outside of each ball. Place rolled candy on a tray and chill until firm, about 4 hours. Keep chilled until serving.

Makes 2 dozen pieces.

Clothespin Cookies

Brad and Marjorie Gessner

Mom and her sister Betty Moody first made these cookies for my cousin's sixteenth birthday party. That was over fifty-five years ago. Mom learned to bake from her Mother Ella Brown. She has baked for every event and organization she and my Dad belonged to. She won "Best of Show" in baking at the Canfield Fair two times and in 1970 represented Mahoning County at the Ohio State Fair for the Ohio Edison State Baking Championship. In the 1960s she appeared on local WFMJ-TV 21's baking show hosted by Margie Marriner. After making macarons for the Historical Society's Cookie Table and Cocktails event, I remarked that my life in the late 60s and early 70s would have been so much better if they had had disposable bags for filling clothespin cookies back then. I remember helping to fill clothespin cookies with an old aluminum plunger frosting tube. It held enough for about a dozen cookies. The disposable pastry bags we use today can fill an entire batch.

INGREDIENTS
CLOTHESPIN PASTRY

1 16-ounce can of Crisco
3 cups flour
3 tablespoons sugar
2 egg yolks
1 ¼ cups water

CLOTHESPIN FILLING

1 cup Crisco
1 cup milk
4 tablespoons flour
2 cups powdered sugar
6 tablespoons marshmallow creme
1 teaspoon vanilla

Also needed: 2 dozen old fashioned wooden clothespins or small dowel rods, 6 x ½-inch.

PREPARATION
CLOTHESPIN PASTRY

Mix flour and sugar, cut in 1/4 of the Crisco; add egg yolks and water, mix as for pie dough. Refrigerate for 2 hours. Roll out dough on a floured board, spread ¼ cup of remaining Crisco over dough, fold 3 times. Refrigerate 1 hour. Repeat this process two more times, using ¼ cup of shortening each time to laminate the dough; refrigerate 1 hour after each time.

Grease your wooden clothespins or dowel rods. Preheat the oven to 425 degrees F.

Roll out ¼ of dough at a time into a 6 x 18-inch rectangle, cut into strips ½-inch by 6 inches. Wrap strips of dough loosely around a greased wooden clothespin or dowel rod, overlap the dough as you roll. Place on ungreased cookie sheets. Repeat the cutting and wrapping with the rest of the dough. Bake at 425 degrees for 5 minutes, reduce heat to 375 degrees for 10 minutes until golden brown. Cool 2–3 minutes and work pastry off the clothespin by squeezing the bottom of the pins together. Be careful as they are very fragile. Leave to cool completely.

CLOTHESPIN FILLING

Cook milk until very warm, stir in flour until thick, set aside to cool. Using a hand mixer, cream Crisco, sugar, marshmallow cream, and vanilla; add flour mixture, beat until consistency of whipped cream. Refrigerate for 15–30 minutes.

Fill cookies from both ends with a cake decorator. Dust with powdered sugar.

Cream Wafers

Sally Palumbo and Chelsey Ludwiczak

Every family wedding we have, my mom makes these traditional cream wafer cookies and fills them with the wedding color. I can remember helping her fill the cookies growing up and looking forward to the challenge of finding unique food colorings (lilac, steel blue, etc.). These cookies are more than a recipe to me—they represent my mom and all the times we spent in her kitchen.

My mom is the one who taught me my love for baking. I can remember coming home from school and having the smell of fresh baked chocolate chip cookies as soon as I walked in the door. I have faint memories being as young as 3 or 4 and helping her scoop cupcakes in a pan. She would make matching aprons for us so we looked like twins. We would both snicker as we would save the "wounded" cookies (those that were burnt or fell apart) for my dad who would happily wait on the sidelines for an imperfectly perfect treat. I'm now 26, and to this day, we still get together to prepare cookies for weddings and look forward to the challenge of finding the perfect sprinkle, coloring, or adornment to match the wedding theme and colors.

I feel my mom's love for the cookie table blossomed after marrying my dad fifty years ago. My dad comes from a strong Italian background, and his family established here in Youngstown in the early 1900s from Buffalo, New York.

The Italian cookie table is more than just a tradition to me. It's a way to show your love for the bride and groom. It's the time you get to spend with family while making the cookies. It's making memories and passing down recipes, creating the backbone of what is The Youngstown Cookie Table.

INGREDIENTS
WAFERS

1 cup butter or margarine, softened
½ cup whipping cream
2 cups flour
Granulated sugar (for coating the wafers)

FILLING

¼ cup soft butter
¾ cup confectioners sugar
1 egg yolk
1 teaspoon vanilla
food coloring, optional

PREPARATION
WAFERS

In a medium bowl, mix butter, whipping cream, and flour thoroughly to form a dough. Wrap in plastic and chill for one hour.

FILLING

In a small bowl, using a hand mixer or whisk, mix the butter, confectioners sugar, egg yolks, and vanilla until the ingredients are combined. If you want to to tint the filling, add a few drops of food coloring and blend until no streaks are visible.

Preheat the oven to 375 degrees F.

On a lightly floured surface, roll dough to ⅛-inch thickness. Using a biscuit or round cookie cutter, cut dough into 1½-inch rounds. Sprinkle granulated sugar on a piece of wax paper, coat rounds on both sides with sugar. Place rounds on ungreased cookie sheets, prick each round three or four times each with a fork.

Bake 5–7 minutes or until lightly puffy. Allow to cool on racks.

When completely cool, spread one generous teaspoon of cream filling onto one of the wafers and then top with another wafer.

Creme de Menthe Brownies

Stacey Adger

These rich, minty brownies won the award for "Best Cocktail Inspired Cookie" at the 2020 Cookie Table and Cocktails event.

INGREDIENTS
BROWNIES

1 ounce (4 squares) Baker's unsweetened chocolate
1 cup butter
4 eggs, beaten
2 cups sugar
1 cup flour
1 teaspoon vanilla

CREME DE MENTHE LAYER

½ cup butter, softened
3 cups powdered sugar
4 tablespoons creme de menthe liqueur
3 tablespoons milk
2 teaspoons peppermint extract
green food coloring

CHOCOLATE GLAZE

4 ounces (1 box) Baker's sweetened chocolate
4 tablespoons butter

PREPARATION

Preheat the oven to 350 degrees F.

Melt chocolate and butter, set aside to cool. Combine eggs and sugar and beat until sugar dissolves. Add flour to eggs and sugar. Add melted chocolate and butter; mix well. Bake in a 9 x 13-inch pan for 25 minutes. Set aside to cool.

Combine powdered sugar with butter; beat in creme de menthe, milk, peppermint extract, and green food coloring. Spread over brownies. Cover and refrigerate until firm.

Melt together chocolate and butter and pour on top of the mint cream layer, spreading and smoothing with spatula. Chill and cut into bars.

Makes about 3 dozen.

Croatian Crescents (Kifli)

Alec Ring

I was born and raised in Youngstown, Ohio, a very ethnic part of the country. My family has been here since the 1930s. Many Italians and Eastern Europeans live here. We have ethnic churches and neighborhoods where all these recipes come alive and traditions are carried through. Every culture has a different name for the same product, but we can agree they are all delicious and are special to each group of people. This crescent cookie (Kifli) is a Croatian cookie, which my Polish grandpa loved and dunked in his coffee, and it is also my favorite cookie.

INGREDIENTS
DOUGH

1/2 cup sugar
1/2 pound unsalted butter, extremely soft but not melted
2 egg whites, unbeaten
1 teaspoon vanilla
3 cups flour
1/2 cup walnuts, ground fine

SUGAR MIXTURE

⅓ cup sugar
1 teaspoon cinnamon

PREPARATION

Preheat the oven to 350 degrees F. Cream the sugar and the butter until combined well. Mix in the egg whites and the vanilla until no streaks appear. Slowly add the flour until a dough forms, try not to overmix. Stir in the ground walnuts; you will have a slightly sandy dough. Scoop out tablespoon-sized balls of dough and, working on a lightly floured surface, curl into small horseshoes. Transfer to a parchment-lined cookie sheet then bake for 20 minutes.

When hot out of the oven, roll cookies in the sugar/cinnamon mixture. Allow to cool completely on racks.

Dreamy Chocolate Bars

Linda Sproul

I've made these delicious Dreamy Chocolate Bars for gatherings, bake sales, and gifts so many times, it's my "signature dessert." My kids ALWAYS ask me for these. This is my mom's signature dessert, too! She found this recipe in a magazine back in 1974 and we still can't get enough of it! Very easy, and oh so good!

Linda Sproul started the Youngstown Cookie Table Facebook group back in 2010 because she looked online and couldn't find anything like it. She wanted to create an online community so people could share photos of their cookie tables, their favorite cookie recipes, and maybe even show a little pride with their Youngstown or eastern Ohio roots. "I didn't think too long or hard about it about it, I just couldn't believe there wasn't a Facebook page, so I created one," she says. The Facebook group currently has approximately 15,000 members from all over the world.

INGREDIENTS
BOTTOM CRUST

1 cup flour
½ cup brown sugar
½ cup (1 stick) cold, unsalted butter, cut up into ¼ inch cubes

TOP LAYER

2 eggs, beaten
1 cup brown sugar
2 tablespoon flour
½ teaspoon baking powder
¼ teaspoon salt
1 teaspoon vanilla
1 12-ounce bag semi-sweet chocolate chips

Preparation

Preheat the oven to 350 degrees F. Liberally grease a 13 x 9 x 2-inch pan.

BOTTOM CRUST

Using a pastry cutter (Linda's preferred method) or your fingers, blend the flour, brown sugar, and butter in a medium bowl until there are no chunks of butter left and the mixture looks like moist crumbs. Using a wooden spoon, blend the ingredients together until it comes together, reaching a pie-dough consistency. Spread dough in an even layer in the greased pan. Put in a 350 degree oven for about 5–8 minutes and bake until dough is slightly browned; it will still be somewhat soft. Take out and set aside.

TOP LAYER

In a medium bowl beat eggs, then mix in sugar, flour, baking powder, and salt. Stir in vanilla and chocolate chips. Pour over browned crust and return pan to oven, baking for 22–25 minutes. Once cool, dust with confectioner's sugar and cut into bars.

Variations: Linda says she has had much success swapping butterscotch chips for the chocolate chips. You just need to call them Dreamy Butterscotch Bars!

Gram Swaney's Potato Chip Cookies

Cynthia Foust

This recipe is from my good friend's beloved Grandma Swaney. She is so remembered for these cookies. They get better after a few days! (If you don't eat them before then.) My friend says everyone in the family makes at least a double or triple batch to have enough for all occasions. I have made these cookies for the Cookie Table and Cocktails event the last seven years. I have made so many wonderful friends because of this cookie recipe!

The original recipe calls for Oleo, because that's probably what was easiest for Gram Swaney to get, but Cynthia now uses butter. You could also substitute margarine if you wanted to.

People who have not ever had a Potato Chip Cookie often ask what they taste like. In testing and tasting this recipe, we determined that it was like the country cousin to a traditional Wedding Cookie, with a bit more texture (from the potato chips, of course) and in a more casual drop cookie format than rolled into a ball. Cynthia was spot on about these cookies getting better with a day or two, but they are still quite delicious if you eat them the same day you bake them. The key is to let them cool completely, as the potato chips get a bit of their structure back and give the cookies a pleasant crispness.

This is not a cookie that you can freeze, but if you were making them for a cookie table, you could easily make them a few days ahead, but hold off on dusting or rolling in powdered sugar until the day they will be served.

Ingredients

2 sticks butter, softened
½ cup sugar
1 teaspoon vanilla
1 cup crushed potato chips (do not crush too fine)
1 1/2 cups flour
½ cup nuts, chopped medium fine
powdered sugar (for rolling or dusting)

Preparation

Preheat the oven to 350 degrees F.

Cream butter and sugar together until fluffy; add vanilla until blended. Add flour, ½ cup at a time, and stir with a wooden spoon. Mix in nuts and crushed potato chips until all are incorporated with the dough, which will be slightly sticky. Drop heaping teaspoonfuls onto an ungreased baking sheet and bake for 10–12 minutes, until the outside edges are golden brown. Remove from the oven and transfer cookies to a cooling rack.

Allow cookies to cool completely and either roll in or dust with powdered sugar. (Original recipe calls for rolling in powdered sugar, which results in a thicker coating.)

Makes about 2 ½ dozen cookies. This recipe is easily doubled.

Grandmother Mary O'Hara Kerrigan's Irish Soda Bread

Betty Kerrigan Winland

Growing up in Youngstown in the 70s, I always thought that the cookie table tradition was reserved for Italians. My maiden name is Kerrigan and my mom's maiden name was McLaughlin, so we are obviously of the Irish ethnicity. So at my wedding in 1982, we had an Irish Soda Bread table. Basically I baked many loaves of my grandmother's recipe that she brought over from County Sligo in the early 1900s and served them with butter.

On another note, I moved to Columbus, Ohio after our wedding and have lived there ever since. Our son Danny, met Alyssa, the daughter of two Youngstown people, Mike DePaola and Patty McBride and they were recently married. You bet that Patty and Mike made sure that there was a cookie table at their reception here. The Columbus people were amazed and thrilled at the selection.

A note about this dough: It is distinctly more batter-like than other soda breads you might have made before. You will not be kneading it before putting the dough into the skillet—it is far too wet for that. And the temperature of the oven at 300 degrees is not a typo. Think of this as a much more "low and slow" version of Irish Soda Bread. But the results are a moist crumb with a golden brown crust.

INGREDIENTS

5 cups flour
1 tablespoon baking powder
1 teaspoon baking soda
1 teaspoon salt
2/3 cup sugar
3 cups raisins
2 beaten eggs
1/2 teaspoon cream of tartar
2 cups buttermilk
2 tablespoon butter, melted

PREPARATION

Soften raisins by soaking them in boiling water for 15 minutes. Drain and set aside.

Preheat the oven to 300 degrees F.

In a large bowl, sift the first 4 ingredients together; add the sugar and raisins. In a separate bowl, stir beaten eggs and cream of tartar together, add the buttermilk and butter. Add the wet ingredients to the dry ingredients and mix well. Dough will be extremely sticky, more like a sticky batter.

Scrape dough into a 10-inch round, greased cast iron skillet, Grandma's way. Bake for 20 minutes. Remove skillet and cut an X on top of the dough, go all the way through to allow fullest rising capacity. (The dough will still be quite wet and tacky, but inserting the knife here does help with the later rise.) Return the skillet to the oven and continue baking for 50 more minutes. To make sure the center is done, test with a knife. Cover with foil if you feel the top is getting too brown. Spread butter over the top while it is still warm. Slice into thick slices and serve with butter.

What's in a Name? Kolachi, Kolache, Nut Rolls and even . . . Potica

One of the staples at many Youngstown holiday celebrations as well as on local cookie tables is the Nut Roll, also locally referred to as Kolachi. This is a yeasted dough, filled with finely ground sweetened nuts, or poppyseeds, sweet cream cheese, or cooked fruits such as apricots or prunes, known as lekvar. It is rolled into a long rectangular shape, ends tucked in, brushed with a beaten egg, pricked with a few holes and baked, and then sliced into thin pieces. The term Kolach comes from the Czech, an originally Old Slavonic word ("kolo") meaning "circle" or "wheel." In Youngstown, various Kolachi recipes have been handed down from Polish, Czech, Hungarian, and other Eastern European bakers, and walked across the street to neighbors and shared with co-workers. It would not be unusual to find Kolachi served at an Italian wedding or at a staff retirement party. You can pick up a "decent" version at the local grocery store and Buttermaid Bakery in Boardman even ships them across the country, to those longing for a taste of home.

But if you do travel around the rest of the country and ask for Kolachi, it can get a bit confusing or tricky. Czechs brought their love of Kolachi to Texas, but there you will find circular pieces of yeasted pastry filled with stewed fruits such as strawberries and sometimes savory items such ground sausage. In the Chicago area, if you ask for a Kolachi you will be served a cookie that Y-towners call Kiffles, or possibly a small round cookie, not unlike those served in Texas, but significantly smaller. In places that had a large Slovenian population, like Cleveland, or Pueblo, Colorado, you might get a blank stare when you ask for Kolachi, but ask for a Potica (pronounced poh-tee-tsuh) and you will get what you were looking for, usually filled with ground walnuts, sometimes with poppyseeds.

No matter what you call it, you know a local delicacy is beloved if it routinely gets served at cookie tables and everyone seems to happily overlook the fact that it is not even a cookie at all.

Kolachi (aka Nut Rolls)

Alec Ring

I am twenty-two years old and have cooked all my life. I come from an Eastern European family with some Italian and Irish roots: Mom is Eastern European and Dad is Irish and Italian. So, I know all about pizzelles and biscotti, etc. When my brother and I were younger, my parents worked a lot so we spent a lot of time over at our grandparents' house (Mom's side). Grandma is Croatian and Grandpa was Polish. All the holidays were complete with the old "hunky" (slang for Eastern European) foods: stuffed cabbage, kolbasi. nut rolls. etc. But through the years, after Grandpa had died, Grandma slowly lost interest in cooking but still wanted the traditions alive. No one else in the family cooked and baked, so I took it upon myself to learn and carry on the traditions. I got all my recipes from Grandma. Every time I cook and bake, I remember all those holidays, all those family gatherings, all those Sunday dinners when we were gathered around Grandma's table laughing and enjoying each other's company. I want to be able to share those with my own wife and kids one day.

INGREDIENTS
DOUGH

Eggs and sour cream should be at room temperature to work best with the yeast.

1/2 cup warm water
1 teaspoon sugar
1 tablespoon active dry yeast
6 cups flour
1 teaspoon salt
1/2 cup sugar
1/2 pound unsalted butter, softened
1 cup sour cream

3 eggs
1 teaspoon vanilla extract
4 tablespoon melted butter, for brushing the dough
1 egg, beaten for brushing the rolls

FILLINGS

Note: All of the measurements below are enough to fill the four rolls with the filling. So if you want to do two rolls with the nut filling and two rolls with the poppyseed, you will want to halve the recipe for each of those fillings. Regardless of the filling, always paint the rolled-out dough with melted butter prior to spreading the filling.

NUT FILLING

1 1/2 pounds walnuts, ground fine, like sawdust (using an old-fashioned grinder is Alec's strong recommendation, he says it is what prevents your nut rolls from bursting, but nuts ground in a food processor with the blade setting works as an option)
2 cups sugar
1 cup warm milk
I teaspoon vanilla extract

Additional flavoring options: Cinnamon, lemon or orange rind, rum or other liquor. Alec likes to use a little lemon rind and vanilla. He says his Grandma just used vanilla.

Mix nuts and sugar. Add enough milk to make a peanut butter-like texture and mix well. Vanilla extract. rum, lemon rind/orange rind, cinnamon, etc any flavor you want can be added now. Divide into four parts, using one for each roll.

POPPY SEED FILLING

1 pound poppy seeds
2 cups sugar
2 tablespoons melted butter
Juice and rind of 1/2 lemon
HOT milk or HOT water, as needed

Mix poppy seeds, sugar, melted butter, and lemon rind. Add lemon juice and blend well. Add enough hot liquid to make a texture like peanut butter. Divide into four parts, using one for each roll.

CHEESE FILLING

2 8-ounce packages of cream cheese, softened
2 eggs
2 tablespoons cornstarch
1/2 cup sugar
2 teaspoons vanilla

Using a hand mixer, beat the cream cheese and add the eggs until combined. Mix in the cornstarch, sugar, and vanilla, blending well.

PREPARATION

Add 1 teaspoon sugar and yeast to warm water (110 degrees to 115 degrees F) and let stand for 10 minutes.

In a large bowl, use your hands to combine the flour, salt, sugar, and butter until mixture resembles coarse breadcrumbs. Make a well in the center of this mixture. In a medium bowl, beat the eggs, sour cream, and vanilla until smooth and pour into the well, along with the yeast.

Blend well with your hands, until the dough is smooth and elastic. Continue kneading the dough until it is smooth and easy to handle and no longer sticky, about 5 minutes.

Lightly oil the dough, place in a lightly oiled bowl; cover with a damp linen, and allow to rise in a warm, draft-free area for 2–3 hours, until it has doubled in size. Don't be alarmed if the dough doesn't rise too quickly and don't rush it. The dough is high in fat (butter, sour cream, and eggs), which makes for a denser dough with a longer rising time. Ultimately, this makes for a lighter finished product but the rise will probably be slow. Using the "proof" setting on your oven might help (if that's an option) or simply put the dough in the oven with the light on. Remember, proofing temp is just about 80 degrees, so you don't want to turn the oven on, it will be too hot.

When the dough has risen, cut it into four equal sections and roll each piece out on a lightly floured board to about 14 x 14 inches square. Make sure that you don't roll the dough too thin or the rolling will be both difficult and floppy. If need be, you can make a slightly smaller square.

Brush the surface of the rolled out dough with about 2 tablespoons melted butter and spread a generous amount of whichever filling you are using. Spread the filling all the way to the edges. Roll up tightly (as if making a jelly roll) and place two rolls on a greased 10 x 15-inch cookie sheet. Cover again with a damp linen cloth and let rise in a warm area for 1 hour.

Paint the tops and sides of the rolls with the beaten eggs, and prick each roll with a fork a few times on top. Bake at 350 for 30–35 minutes, until golden and hollow when tapped. Remove from the oven, let cool on the trays they were baked on, and brush tops and sides with melted butter while still hot. Cool completely overnight, the texture and flavor are best on the second day.

Kourabiedes (Greek Butter Cookies)

Anna Pitinii Hood

Some people think of these as classic Greek Wedding Cookies, while others associate them with Christmastime. For the many members of the Pitinii family, they might show up at both!

INGREDIENTS

1 pound salted butter, softened
1/2 cup powdered sugar
1 egg yolk
1 jigger whiskey
1 teaspoon vanilla
4 cups sifted flour
3 cups powdered sugar

PREPARATION

Preheat the oven to 350 degrees F.

Beat soft butter and powdered sugar until creamy, about 15 minutes. Add egg yolk, vanilla, and whiskey until well blended. Gradually add flour to make a soft dough. Try not to overmix the dough.

Pinch off a piece of dough and shape into a round, or crescent. Place on an ungreased cookie sheet, one inch apart. Bake for 15-20 minutes until very pale brown. Do not over bake, they will not brown on top. Allow to cool slightly before removing from the cookie trays. On a clean and cool cookie tray (or a cooling rack with paper towels or something underneath to catch the falling sugar), sprinkle powdered sugar over the cookies. Place each cookie in a small paper cup. Store in an airtight container. Do not store in the refrigerator or freeze.

To make these cookies ahead of time:

Let the baked cookies cool completely, WITHOUT the powdered sugar step. Store in the fridge or freeze in an airtight container. When ready to finish the cookies, bring to room temperature. Put in a 300 degree oven to warm. Finish with the powdered sugar step.

Makes about 5 dozen cookies.

Lemon Lavender Love Cookies

Stephanie Winegardner

I'm a novice baker. I've never been good at it and it was always intimidating. My mom (Rachelle Benchwick) and sister (Carissa Benchwick) have always been the family bakers—they are also both Youngstown Cookie Table winners! My niece, Sage Benchwick, has won Youngest Baker twice! In 2019, they convinced me to submit a cookie to the competition. I really did it to socialize and learn something new. I love the combination of lemon and lavender and wanted to put it into a cookie. I burned every recipe I found! Finally, my nurse brain shifted into gear and I researched how to make my own cookie recipe. It wasn't until I learned the chemistry behind each ingredient that baking made sense. So, I played around with different ingredients until I came up with this recipe for Lemon Lavender Love Cookies.

INGREDIENTS

1 tablespoon dried culinary lavender
1 teaspoon finely grated lemon zest
1/3 cup granulated sugar
1/2 cup unsalted butter softened
1/2 tsp vanilla extract
1 egg yolk
1 tablespoon lavender syrup* (If you can find it. It's not necessary)
1 tablespoon lemon juice
1–1 1/2 cup all-purpose flour (depending on how sticky)
1/4 teaspoon salt
1 teaspoon baking powder

Preparation

Preheat the oven to 325 degrees F.

Place 1 tablespoon of the granulated sugar, dried lavender, and lemon zest in a mortar and grind lightly with the pestle. This releases the lavender and lemon oils. Make sure you smell it . . . this is my favorite part!

Place lavender mixture in a large bowl with remaining sugar and butter. Cream together until smooth. Add vanilla, egg yolk, lemon juice, and lavender syrup (if using). Add dry ingredients to the butter mixture until it forms a dough. Do not over mix! I start with 1 cup flour and slowly add 1 tablespoon more at a time until not sticky. Shape into a log and wrap tightly in plastic wrap.

Refrigerate for 30 minutes or freeze for later use.

Line a large baking sheet with parchment paper. Slice dough into ½-inch thick discs. I like to decorate the tops with some pieces of dried lavender.

Bake cookies for 12–14 minutes until lightly browned around the edges. Remove from the oven and transfer to a wire rack.

* I get my lavender syrup from a local coffee shop that makes it in house. Don't use a fake lavender syrup or essential oil, because it may taste like soap. If you want a stronger lavender taste or don't have the syrup add more dried lavender.

Makes about 24 cookies.

London Fog Shortbread

Rachelle Rembowski Benchwick

Rachelle entered this cookie in the 2020 Youngstown Cookie Table and Cocktails contest, under "Best Unusual Ingredient" category, and the judges honored it with First Place.

INGREDIENTS

1 cup butter, softened (2 sticks)
⅔ cup powdered sugar
1 tablespoon vanilla bean paste or vanilla extract
2 tablespoons loose-leaf Earl Grey tea (about 5 teabags)
1 ¾ cup flour
sanding sugar or turbinado sugar for sprinkling

PREPARATION

Using a hand or electric mixer, cream together the butter and powdered sugar until fluffy. Add vanilla and tea leaves. Add the flour and mix by hand until the dough comes together. Wrap the dough in plastic and put in the refrigerator to chill for at least 30 minutes.

Preheat the oven to 350 degrees F.

On a lightly floured surface, roll the dough out to about ½ inch thick. Cut shapes out using desired cookie cutter and place on a cookie sheet covered with parchment paper. Sprinkle with sanding or turbinado sugar. Return cookies to the refrigerator to chill an additional 10–20 minutes. Bake at 350 degrees for 12–14 minutes; cool on wire racks.

Margaret Mary's Molasses Cookies

Grace Murray

My grandma used to make these molasses cookies when we would visit her house on Hilton Avenue in downtown Youngstown. We were never allowed to play outside when we visited because she lived in a pretty rough neighborhood, but we still loved to visit and share in her sweet tooth.

I got married this past December and these cookies were present at our gigantic cookie table. She wasn't able to be there as she passed many years ago, but with the help of the cookies, it definitely felt like she was there.

If you want to make the cookies just as she did, be sure to burn the bottoms of them. She was always playing cards and would forget to take them out of the oven. Though, after having six kids of her own and ten-plus grandchildren, I don't think she minded anything burnt. She was just happy to put some food in her system.

INGREDIENTS

¾ cup Crisco, room temperature
1 cup packed brown sugar
1 large egg
¼ cup of molasses
2 ¼ cups all-purpose flour
2 teaspoons baking soda
½ teaspoon salt
1 ½ teaspoon cinnamon
1 ½ teaspoon ginger
½ teaspoon ground cloves

PREPARATION

Put the Crisco and brown sugar in a large bowl. Using a standing mixer, beat until smooth.

Add the egg and molasses to the mixture making sure to scrape the sides of the bowl clean.

Mix all of the dry ingredients together in a separate bowl. Once well mixed, add them to the wet ingredients and beat until combined. You want to make sure you don't over-beat the batter, as it will result in tough-to-chew cookies. Place the batter in the fridge for 2–3 hours.

Preheat the oven to 350 degrees F. Using a teaspoon, scoop the dough and roll into 1 ½-inch balls and place on a baking sheet.

Bake the cookies for 9–10 minutes or just until the tops of the cookies start to crack. Once you see the cracks, take them out of the oven, or they will burn.

Makes about 30 cookies.

Mom's Peanut Butter Cookies with a Twist

Rachelle Rembowski

In 2017 I entered this recipe in the Youngstown Cookie Table and Cocktails contest, the category was "Original Cookie with a Twist." So I used my mom's peanut butter cookie recipe (I still have it, written in her own handwriting) and added a Fun Size Snickers bar cut in thirds, a drizzle of chocolate, and chopped honey roasted peanuts. I ended up winning third place! The reason I entered it in the Cookies and Cocktails contest is because the event reminds me of a traditional Youngstown wedding: polka band, Italian food, and a beautiful cookie table, all made from friends and family, Such wonderful memories.

Also, I now call this my "Man Cookie." Men who say they don't eat sweets will request this cookie. And on a practical note: after every holiday stores have plenty of Fun Size Snickers bars on sale. So I buy them at half-price and freeze them until I need them for these cookies.

INGREDIENTS

1 cup sugar
1 cup brown sugar
1 cup peanut butter (smooth)
1 cup margarine or butter, softened
2 eggs
1 teaspoon vanilla
2 teaspoons baking soda
3 cups flour
20 Snickers "Fun Size" candy bars
½ cup sugar (for coating)
¼ cup honey-nut-roasted peanuts

PREPARATION

Preheat the oven to 350 degrees F.

Cream sugars, butter, and peanut butter. Add eggs and vanilla, beat until smooth. Add flour and baking soda, mix well.

Cut Snickers bars into thirds. Scoop a well-rounded tablespoon of cookie dough and press the Snickers slice into the center of the dough. Gently form a ball around the candy; no part of the Snickers should be showing or sticking out. Roll ball in sugar and set at least 1 inch apart from each cookie on an ungreased cookie sheet.

Bake cookies for 10–12 minutes, until they are a pale brown. Remove from the oven and cool on wire racks.

Melt chocolate chips in the microwave (time will vary for different ovens) or double boiler. Using a small spoon, drizzle each cookie with criss-cross lines of melted chocolate and sprinkle with the chopped nuts.

Yola's Nut Rolls

Marie McNulty

This Nut Roll recipe is what my mom, Yolanda "Viola" McNulty was famous for. Luckily, I studied her and I am now able to make them almost as well as she did.

INGREDIENTS
DOUGH

1 ½ cups lukewarm milk
3 ounces cake yeast (1 ½ cakes, sold at 2 ounces each—Marie uses Red Star brand)
¼ cup sugar
10 cups flour
1 pound sweet butter (cold, cut into cubes)
1 teaspoon salt
12 egg yolks
1 cup sour cream
beaten egg
melted butter

FILLING

12 egg whites
3 cups sugar
3 pounds walnuts (finely ground with old fashioned tabletop meat grinder, or you can use a food processor)

Beat egg whites in a cold bowl of a standing mixer, slowly at first. Once the eggs become frothy, add the cream of tartar. Turn up the speed until they become white and start to form peaks. Gradually add the sugar and beat until stiff peaks form. Gently stir in the ground nuts.

PREPARATION
DOUGH

Dissolve the yeast in lukewarm water with ¼ cup sugar. Let it rise! It should take between 5 and 10 minutes and be bubbly and appear puffy at the top.

Sift flour and salt in a large bowl. Blend butter pieces into the flour using a pastry cutter.

Add sour cream, egg yolks, and yeast mixture (after it has risen) into flour. Stir, then work the dough with your hands.

Knead dough for about 10 minutes.

Place dough in a large oiled bowl, cover loosely with plastic wrap and 2-3 clean dish towels. Set the bowl in a warm spot (such as an oven with the light turned on) and let sit undisturbed until the dough doubles in size, about two hours. After it has risen, cut the dough into eight equal parts. Cover and let rest for 10 minutes.

Roll each piece of dough to about a 14-inch-wide rectangle—no bigger or you will not have enough filling.

Using an offset spatula, spread filling onto dough. (You will be using an eighth of the filling for each roll.) Just enough to cover the dough. Do not overfill.

With the filling-covered dough placed horizontally in front of you, start at one end and roll dough away from you (similar to rolling cinnamon rolls). Tuck in each of the ends of the dough and make sure the seams are pinched closed.

Place rolled dough on a lightly greased cookie sheet; repeat with other rolls but do not put more than two rolls per cookie sheet. Cover rolls with clean dishcloths and let rise for one hour.
Once they are risen, brush each roll with beaten egg and use a knife to cut small slits into each to vent the rolls as they bake.

Place rolls in the oven and bake at 350 degrees for 25 minutes.

After taking them out of the oven, place on cooling racks and brush with melted butter.

Once completely cool, wrap each roll in plastic wrap and then in foil to keep fresh.

They freeze beautifully for up to six months.

Makes 8 Nut Rolls.

Orange Cookies

Mary Stano Musick and Maryann Musick Kress

My mom, Mary Stano Musick, got this recipe from her very dear friend, Ann Hiryok. She helped Ann with her catering business, and this cookie became a staple for weddings and for us.

The cookbook title was "Grandma Mary's Favorites." I made thirteen copies—one for mom, one for each of the eight grandchildren, and four for my siblings and me. Considering I was working at the time, it took me a couple years to complete. My mom knew I was putting some of her recipes together, but she didn't know to what extent. Besides the recipes I knew were our favorites (pirogues, stuffed cabbage, lots of cookies), I asked each of my siblings and grandkids if they had a special favorite. I decided to add a little biography of mom at the end of each section throughout the cookbook. The biography included birth, her childhood, working, wedding, along with notable events or occurrences during her life, plus lots of pictures of her at all ages. Every time I was with my mom, I would do a little interview and ask her specific questions or ask her to elaborate on something I knew a little about. I wanted the grandkids to be able to pick up the cookbook, bake their favorite recipe, and also be able to read about their grandmother and really know her. I gave everyone their cookbook for Christmas, December 2011. My mom was 94.

This is a classic citrus-infused cookie that is delicate and airy. Maryann Musick Kress, who grew up in Warren, Ohio, collected all of the recipes from her mother Mary Stano Musick and put them in binders and gifted them to all of the grandchildren as well as her four siblings. This is one of their favorites.

DOUGH

½ teaspoon baking soda
½ teaspoon baking powder
2 cups flour
½ teaspoon salt
⅔ cup shortening or butter, softened
¾ cup sugar
1 egg, beaten
½ cup orange juice
2 tablespoons grated orange rind

ICING

1 pound (16-ounce) box of of powdered sugar
3 tablespoons softened butter
2 tablespoons orange juice (from one orange)
2 tablespoons grated orange rind

Optional: a piece of candied orange peel or orange sugar crystal on top for decoration

PREPARATION

Preheat the oven to 375 degrees F.

In a medium bowl, mix together the first four dry ingredients. In a separate bowl, cream together sugar, shortening (or butter), and egg. Stir in orange juice and orange rind. Add dry ingredients to the wet and mix together well. Drop teaspoonfuls of the dough onto a lightly greased cookie sheet, 1½ inches apart. Bake for 9–10 minutes, then remove from the oven and cool on a wire rack.

For icing, mix all of the ingredients in a bowl until blended. Spread icing on top of cooled cookies.

Pecan Petites

Carol Brungardt Mound

I grew up on South Dunlap, in Youngstown. I learned how to bake and cook from Grandma Simko (from Czechoslovakia) and my mom, Millie. They made everything from scratch and were both fantastic cooks and bakers. These Pecan Petites were a recipe of my mom's, they are a longtime family favorite. I almost always quadruple the recipe.

INGREDIENTS

1 cup margarine or butter
¼ cup sugar
1 teaspoon vanilla
2 cups flour
1 cup chopped pecans
powdered sugar for coating

PREPARATION

Preheat the oven to 325 degrees F. Cream margarine/butter and sugar until light and fluffy. Blend in vanilla. Add flour; mix well. Stir in nuts. Shape the dough into balls by the rounded teaspoonful; place on an ungreased cookie sheet. Bake for 20 minutes. Cool slightly and roll in the powdered sugar.

Makes approximately 3 dozen cookies.

The Cookie Table Gets Competitive

When someone bakes exceptionally large amounts of cookies for a loved one's wedding, there's certainly a bit of pride (and even some bragging rights) that goes along with it, but nobody wins a prize or has a panel of judges sampling your cookies. That all changes once a year when the Cookie Table and Cocktails event takes place in Youngstown. The Mahoning Valley Historical Society puts on a gala that feels much like a wedding (polka band, Italian food, a decorated hall) except the cookie table has a twist. Bakers donate eight dozen cookies (and in return receive a free ticket to the event) and their hard work, creativity, and overall baking chops are judged by a select panel of cookie tasters. Categories include: Best Cocktail Inspired Cookie, Best Use of an Unusual Ingredient, Best Traditional Cookie, and Best Decorated Cookie. They also give a Judges Choice Award and honor the youngest and oldest bakers. It's a hot ticket in Youngstown: the 2020 Cookie Table and Cocktails event sold out and filled the social hall at Our Lady of Mount Carmel Basilica. Several of the recipes included in this cookbook are former winners and we're proud to have them in our mix.

Pecan Pie Bars

Margaret Trickett-Healey and Jessica Trickett

Margaret made these bars for our staff team for Youngstown's Relay for Life in 2004. Judges at the event awarded them the "Best Late Night Snack" prize. Margaret was always baking for her large group of family and friends.

Submitted by the Mahoning Valley Historical Society, which organizes the popular Cookie Table and Cocktails event each year, this extra decadent recipe comes from Margaret Trickett-Heally (1924-2007) whose daughter Jessica, is a curator at MVHS.

INGREDIENTS
CRUST

3 cups flour
¾ cups sugar
½ tsp salt
1 cup cold butter (2 sticks)

FILLING

4 eggs, beaten
1 ½ cups sugar
1 ½ cups corn syrup
¼ cup melted butter
1 ½ teaspoons vanilla
2 ½ cups chopped pecans

Preparation

For the crust: combine flour, sugar, and salt. Cut in butter until crumbly. Press into the bottom and up sides of a 9 x 13-inch greased pan. Bake at 350 for 10–12 minutes.

For the filling: mix all of the ingredients; pour over the par-baked crust. Bake for 25–30 minutes, or until the center is almost firm. Cool on a wire rack. Cut into small bars and place in paper cups. Refrigerate until serving.

Note: If making these for a special event, it's best to make them at least 24 hours in advance so that all of the ingredients have time to firm up; 48 hours prior is even better.

Pecan Tassies

Stacey Adger

I was born and raised in Youngstown. My father worked in various steel mills to raise money to support the family, mom stayed at home. I started cooking when I was young, being the eldest of four girls. I was lucky to be old enough to understand the importance of food and things that tasted good and provided comfort. I remember some of my older cousins reminiscing, talking about the different desserts and foods older members of the family would make and that always caught my attention. There were certain foods like that traditional Christmas fruitcake, peach cobbler, or the German chocolate cake that were always a constant in the house. By doing research on different family members, I learned that a great aunt was one of the cooks for one of the wealthier families on Wick Avenue and started a small bakery which served some of the wealthier families on the North side. Drawing on my African, Gullah Geechee, Creole, and European heritage, meals and desserts are always an adventure.

INGREDIENTS
CREAM CHEESE PASTRY

1 cup butter, softened
6 ounces cream cheese, softened
¼ teaspoon salt
2 cups all-purpose flour

PECAN FILLING

3 eggs
1 cup light corn syrup
1 cup sugar
2 teaspoons vanilla (preferably Mexican)
2 tablespoons butter, melted
2 ¼ cups finely chopped pecans

PREPARATION
Preheat the oven to 350 degrees F.

CREAM CHEESE PASTRY

Cream together butter and cream cheese in a large bowl with an electric mixer; add salt. Gradually add flour and beat just until combined. Shape pastry dough into two balls; chill for at least 20 to 30 minutes or until dough is easy to handle.

Divide dough into 60 small balls. Press each one into bottoms and up sides of 1 3/4 x 1-inch muffin cups. Set aside.

PECAN FILLING

Beat eggs slightly with a fork in a medium bowl. Stir in corn syrup, sugar, butter, and vanilla until well blended.

Spoon 1 heaping teaspoon pecans into each pastry-lined cup; top with about 1 tablespoon filling mixture.

Bake tarts at 350°F for 15 to 20 minutes or until lightly browned and a cake tester inserted comes out clean. Cool in pans for 10 minutes. Remove from pans using a thin knife and cool completely on wire racks.

Yields about 5 dozen tarts.

Petticoat Tails

Stacey Adger

This recipe is adapted from my mom's fifty-plus-year-old Betty Crocker Cookbook. *I usually make these cookies and use either wintergreen flavoring as instructed in the original recipe or peppermint or spearmint. You can also do simply vanilla or almond, or almost any flavor. I changed up the method a bit too. Rather than cutting off slices from a rolled out log of dough, I prefer to scoop out the dough and form it into balls, and then press each with the bottom of a glass.*

The *Betty Crocker Cookbook* had a side note for this recipe that provided a bit of historical context: "This recipe was brought from France to Scotland by Mary, Queen of Scots. The French name, 'Petits Gateaux Tailles,' means 'little cakes cut off.' But the name came to be pronounced as it sounded to the Scotch and English—'Petticoat Tails.'"

INGREDIENTS

1 cup butter, softened
1 cup powdered sugar
1 teaspoon flavoring of your choice (wintergreen, vanilla, almond, etc.)
2 ½ cups flour
¼ teaspoon salt

PREPARATION

Mix together butter, powdered sugar, and flavoring. Stir in flour and salt. Mix thoroughly with your hands until a dough is formed.

Chill for 30 minutes.

Preheat the oven to 350 degrees F.

Scoop out dough and form ¾-inch balls. Using the back of a flat-bottomed glass, press into the balls until flattened into a disc about ⅛ of an inch thick. Transfer to an ungreased baking sheet.

Bake 8–10 minutes until lightly browned.

Makes about 5 dozen cookies.

Pizzelle

Ange and Vince Guerrieri

This is my Grandmother Ange's Pizzelle recipe, which she got from her aunt, Mary Lariccia. (My wife just uses the one that came with the iron.) True story: my grandfather died the day after Grandma's seventieth birthday. The last thing he bought her was a new pizzelle iron. (Sure beats the hell out of the time he bought her a lawn mower for their anniversary.)

Vince Guerrieri, who submitted this recipe, is one of the contributor's to the first edition of *Car Bombs to Cookie Tables*, Belt Publishing's Youngstown anthology. He's a native of the west side of Youngstown and a graduate of Chaney High School and Bowling Green University. He's the author of two books and spent fifteen years in newspapers. He currently lives with his wife and daughter in suburban Cleveland.

INGREDIENTS

12 eggs
3 cups sugar
2 cups neutral oil such as canola
4 teaspoons vanilla extract
10 cups flour
7 teaspoons baking powder

PREPARATION

Beat eggs until smooth and frothy. Add sugar, beat some more. Add oil and vanilla (or different flavoring, such as anise or lemon). Slowly add the flour and baking powder. Mix well; the dough will be sticky, almost batter-like. Turn on pizzelle iron, rub with oil if need be. Using a teaspoon, scoop out to make sticky dough balls about an inch in diameter and place on the hot pizzelle pan, in the center of each section. Check the directions on your pizzelle iron as some vary slightly in size and you might need more or less dough.

Variation: For chocolate pizzelles, add in three tablespoons each of sugar and cocoa powder. (Vince's wife Shannon adds two tablespoons of cocoa powder and one of espresso powder, plus the three tablespoons of sugar.)

This is a large recipe—Vince describes it as making "about a dozen dozen." It is easily halved.

Raspberry Tarts

Marjorie and Brad Gessner

These are tarts my mother, Marjorie Gessner (who will be celebrating her ninety-fourth birthday this year) has been making for years. They have a great flavor from the brown sugar in the dough. Mom will only make them if she has black raspberry filling; I use the red raspberry. My grandmother was born in Youngstown in 1894 and taught my mother how to cook and bake. My mother and her two sisters could and did bake everything—homemade wedding cakes and cookies, pies for all holidays. I think I was in college before I realized brownies could be made from a box. When I was six my mother had my brother and I baking for the Men's Baking competition at the Canfield Fair; she and my sister competed in the regular divisions. For years my mother and aunt and cousins would bake for every family function, especially weddings and graduations. (Youngstown graduations also have a cookie table tradition.) In 1960, for a fundraiser for my brother's elementary school PTA, my mother compiled her favorite wedding cookie recipes and made a cookie booklet that the PTA sold. These raspberry tarts were one of the recipes included in the booklet. Years later when my brother was in high school the Band Parents club sold her book again.

A note about the dough and the tart pans: as Brad points out, the dough for these tarts has a high brown sugar content, so that it comes out darker with a nubbly, rich texture. It results in a lovely and unique pastry that is something of a tart dough-cookie dough hybrid.

Brad sent the following notes on the pans he uses for these mini tarts: "I use several old aluminum pans that have twelve mini tarts on each. The brand is Comet Aluminum. They were given to me by a lady named Emma Blackstone who was just an amazing baker. She recently passed away at the age of ninety-eight and her pans still look brand new. Those pans, the widest part of the top is just over 1 ½ inches and the bottom narrow part is 1 ¼. They are ⅞ inches deep."

PASTRY FOR TARTS

2 cups brown sugar
1 cup butter (2 sticks) chilled, cut into smaller pieces
3 eggs
4 cups flour
2 teaspoons baking soda
2 teaspoons cream of tartar

FILLING

For the filling we normally use canned pie filling or filling from Rulli Brothers grocery in Austintown. Sometimes we have made our filling with black raspberries, sugar, cornstarch, and lemon juice, but when you are baking for a Youngstown wedding, the volume of cookies needed usually leads you to use commercial filling.

HOMEMADE RASPBERRY FILLING

¼ cup cold water
3 tablespoons cornstarch
4 pints fresh raspberries (or 4 cups frozen)
3 cups sugar
4 tablespoons lemon juice

RASPBERRY FILLING

Combine cornstarch and water in a medium saucepan, stirring until smooth. Stir in sugar, raspberries and lemon juice. Cook over medium-low heat, stirring occasionally for 10–15 minutes, until thickened. Set aside to cool.

TARTS

Preheat the oven to 350 degrees F.

Cream the butter and sugar until fluffy. Add eggs one at a time until well combined. Slowly add the remaining dry ingredients, until a dough is formed, but do not overwork the dough.

On a lightly floured surface, roll dough out ¼ inch thick. Cut circles from the dough and gently press into tart pans. Fill each tart shell half full with raspberry filling. Cut additional small circles from the same dough and lay on top of filled tart shells.

Bake for 25 minutes, remove tarts from the pan, and turn them upside down to cool. Turn tarts back over and sprinkle with powdered sugar.

Makes 4 to 5 dozen tarts

Romanian Cornuletes

Robert J. Craciun, Sr

This cookie recipe was adapted from the *Pofta Buna Cookbook: The Romanian Way of Cooking*. *Pofta buna* means "good appetite" in Romanian. The cookbook was first published in 1957 by the Romanian Orthodox Church of Youngstown, and was revised in 1989. Most of the members of the church are from Romania, services are still held in the Romanian language and according to Robert and his wife, Marguerite, the church provides a lot for those new to this country: family, fellowship resources, etc. They made sure to mention that the church dinners are "true Romanian food."

A note about the dough: Romanian cornulete recipes vary by region to region and also by whatever fats are locally available, such as sour cream, lard, or Farmer's Cheese. This original recipe used a pound of oleo! When Robert started using this recipe he decided to switch to using butter for flavor and texture. The shapes of finished cornuletes vary as well. They might look like diamond-shaped kiffles, or rolled crescents. Marguerite noted that Robert folds each cookie so that it looks like a mini hand pie. "Robert folds them over but I guess they also can be filled and rolled and made into a crescent. Robert also makes them a little bigger than a walnut. The church ladies said they were bigger than traditional, but they disappeared quickly."

INGREDIENTS
DOUGH

2 8-ounce packages of cream cheese, softened
1 pound butter, softened
6 cups flour
1 lemon rind, grated
1 orange rind, grated
egg, beaten for brushing on dough
powdered sugar for dusting

NUT FILLING

1 ½ pound finely ground walnuts (6 cups)
¾ cup milk
¾ cup honey
8 tablespoons (1 stick) melted butter
½ cup sugar
1 tablespoon walnut extract (optional)
grated rind of one lemon

PREPARATION
NUT FILLING

Gently boil milk; add honey, nuts, butter, sugar, and walnut extract (if using). Add a little milk if the filling is too thick.

DOUGH

Cream the butter and cream cheese together. Add the flour 2 cups at a time. Sprinkle in the grated lemon and orange. Using your hands, blend everything together and make sure that the citrus gets evenly distributed in the dough. Divide the dough into three pieces, and wrap each in plastic wrap. Put in the refrigerator overnight to chill.

Two Methods For Rolling Out The Dough

Robert's Half Moon Shape

Pinch off dough into about 165 balls the size of walnuts. Roll each ball out on a powdered-sugared board, so that you have a small circle of dough, about 2 inches in diameter; fill the middle of the circle with a scant teaspoon of preserves or nut filling. Fold over to create a half moon shape and pinch along the rounded edge to bring the two layers of dough together. Brush tops with beaten eggs. Place on a greased cookie sheet. Bake for 20 to 25 minutes at 350 degrees. Sprinkle with powdered sugar when cool.

Traditional Crescent Shape

On a floured surface, roll one piece of the dough at a time into a 10-inch circle, about ¼-inch thick. This is like making pizza. Using a pizza cutter, cut the dough into 12 wedges. At the base of every slice (triangle) add a dollop of the nut filling and roll the dough towards the center of the circle, to form a crescent. Place each rolled crescent on an ungreased baking sheet. Repeat with the remaining two pieces of dough and filling. Brush tops with beaten eggs. Bake for 15–20 minutes at 350 degrees. Cool on wire racks; once cooled, roll in or sprinkle with powdered sugar.

A Note About Fats

Many of the recipes in this cookbook come from fifty, seventy, even one hundred years ago. Some are even older than that! Just as the cookie table tradition was formed around families not being able to afford a costly wedding cake, the fats used in many of these recipes have changed depending on what was affordable, what has been available, and then at a certain point, the preferred flavor or texture. Crisco was introduced in 1911 (and heavily marketed to American housewives) and became the popular choice for many home cooks because it was shelf stable, tasteless, and actually cheaper than lard (unless you were butchering your own pigs). Originally made from cottonseed oil, Crisco later changed to a blend of soy, palm, and canola oils. Many people use the term "shortening" and Crisco interchangeably, but the term shortening is broad and includes any fats that are solid at room temperature, including lard and margarine.

During World War II, butter was scarce and Oleomargarine, an oil-based alternative invented by a French chemist in 1869, was often what you used because it was all there was. Another thing to keep in mind is that with many of these recipes, home bakers were preparing quantities for a very large crowd; whether that was for an upcoming wedding or Christmastime or just a large extended family of many generations. That is still the case when baking cookies for a cookie table today and could inform the fats one might choose to employ. In the end, most bakers are going to choose a fat that is accessible and performs best in whatever it is they are creating. Baklava would not be Baklava without butter and Pizzelles are overwhelmingly made with a neutral oil. When testing the recipes for this cookbook, we used the fat that was listed. If the option of using margarine or butter was indicated, we used butter.

Seven Layer Bars
Judy Rohrbaugh

Judy Rohrbaugh grew up in Youngstown but has lived in Salt Lake City for the past twelve years. For the 2020 Cookie Table and Cocktails event, Judy carried eight dozen of these Seven Layer Bars in her luggage from Salt Lake City to Youngstown, so that they could be served on the table, along with the more than 8,000 other cookies. They are both a family favorite and a tried and true classic for a cookie table. They travel well (obviously) and are open to an infinite variety of variations, a few which Judy has provided below.

INGREDIENTS

1 stick butter, melted
1 ½ cup graham cracker crumbs
1 cup semi-sweet chocolate chips
1 cup butterscotch chips
1 cup shredded coconut, sweetened
1 cup chopped pecans
1 14-ounce can sweetened condensed milk

PREPARATION

Preheat the oven to 325 degrees F. Grease the bottom and sides of a 9 x 13-inch pan. Melt butter and, if need be, break graham crackers into crumbs. Mix together in a bowl until combined. Spread mixture into the bottom of the pan; pat down evenly. Sprinkle the chocolate chips, then the butterscotch chips, shredded coconut, and chopped pecans, in that order. Do not stir or spread! Drizzle the sweetened condensed milk evenly over the entire pan.

Bake for 30 minutes. Remove from the oven and allow to cool completely. Cut into 1-inch squares; a pizza cutter is ideal for a clean cut.

Makes approximately 4 dozen.

Variations:
Use cinnamon graham crackers or chocolate Teddy Grahams to make crumb.

Use peanut butter or salted caramel chips instead of butterscotch chips.

Use unsweetened coconut instead of sweetened.

Use walnuts, hazelnuts or almonds instead of pecans.

Snowballs

Amy Sopko

I first learned to bake in restaurant management classes at the Mahoning County JVS. A few years ago a few of us PTA ladies got together and started baking as gifts for friends and family. We baked for weeks. We made and baked over 10,000 cookies! Then as each year passed we did it less because of schedules. I'm a stay-at-home mom of two girls; this is their favorite cookie. Some call them Butter Balls, but my girls call them Snowballs because it was December the first time I made them about ten years ago. Baking is my passion. I'm no professional, but I have been told my Snowballs are the best. I love spreading cheer even if it's through the belly!

These cookies are indeed close to a Butter Ball, but Amy's version adds almond extract and, true to their name, calls for two coatings of powdered sugar—to make sure there's lots of the white stuff.

INGREDIENTS

1/2 cup powdered sugar, sifted
1 cup butter, softened
2 teaspoons vanilla
3 teaspoons almond extract
2 cups all-purpose flour, sifted
1/4 teaspoon salt
1 cup finely chopped walnuts
1 cup of powdered sugar

Preparation

Preheat the oven to 350 degrees F.

In a large bowl combine powdered sugar, butter, and vanilla. Blend well. Stir in flour, nuts, and salt until dough holds together. You may have to finish by using your hands. Scoop or shape the dough into 1-inch balls; place on ungreased or parchment paper-lined cookie sheets.

Bake for 18–20 minutes until set but not brown. Immediately transfer cookies to wire racks. Cool slightly for 3–5 minutes, and roll in powdered sugar. Put back on the racks, allow cookies to cool completely, then roll one more time in powdered sugar. Store in an airtight container.

Makes approximately 48 cookies.

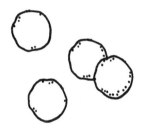

Soft Molasses Cookies

Helen Bedford

This recipe was submitted by Pamela Spies, archivist at the Mahoning Valley Historical Society. She forwarded a photo of a spattered recipe card with the following message: "Here's a recipe that makes soft cut-out cookies that can be plain or decorated. It is a recipe from an old family friend that matched up to what my mom remembers her grandmother making back in the 1940s-1950s."

INGREDIENTS

1 cup molasses (darker molasses will provide a fuller flavor, that's what Pamela prefers)
1 cup shortening (Crisco)
1 cup sour milk or buttermilk
1 cup brown sugar
1 teaspoon salt
2 teaspoons cinnamon
4 teaspoons baking soda
5 cups of flour

PREPARATION

Preheat oven to 350 degrees F.

Blend all of the ingredients in a large bowl until a stiff dough forms. Wrap in plastic and chill in the refrigerator overnight. Roll out to about ¼-inch thick and cut with a round biscuit or cookie cutter. Place on an ungreased cookie sheet and bake for 8-10 minutes.

Optional: decorations such as sprinkles or Cinnamon Imperials can be sprinkled on the dough before baking, or the icing of your choice can be used after the cookies have baked and cooled.

Spiced Chocolate Shortbread Heart Cookies

Karen Schubert

When I was young, my mom used to tease me that my wedding would be potluck and "bring your own cookie." I didn't actually grow up in Youngstown, so I didn't get the joke. When I moved here and saw my first cookie table, I couldn't believe my happiness. And the lovely little guest bags that invite us to take some home? What a gift.

INGREDIENTS

2 cups flour
1/2 cup unsweetened cocoa
1 teaspoon cinnamon
1/2 teaspoon ground ginger
1/4 teaspoon each: cloves, mace, nutmeg, baking powder, salt
1 cup butter (2 sticks) at room temperature
1 cup powdered sugar
1 teaspoon vanilla
powdered sugar for sprinkling

PREPARATION

Sift flour, cocoa, spices, baking powder, and salt in a medium bowl. Beat butter, powdered sugar, and vanilla in a large bowl until fluffy. On low speed, add the flour mixture to the butter mixture until just blended. You can use a wooden spoon or even your hands to bring the dough together. Between two pieces of wax paper, roll out the dough to a thickness of about ½ inch. Refrigerate several hours or overnight.

Preheat the oven to 350 degrees F.

Remove the top sheet of wax paper. Using a 2-inch heart-shaped cookie cutter, cut out dough and place on lightly buttered cookie sheet. Reroll scraps and repeat cutting. Prick the dough on the cut cookies 2 or 3 times with fork tines, then bake about 20 minutes until the cookies are firm to the touch. Let cool on a wire rack. Sprinkle cooled cookies with confectioners' sugar.

Makes about 30 cookies.

Stained Glass Cookies

Sage Benchwick

The Benchwick family could possibly be the eastern Ohio version of the Von Trapp Family Singers, except the Benchwick talents are apparently in the kitchen, whipping up baked goods. Their skills are best demonstrated each year with their participation and success in the annual Cookie Table and Cocktails baking contest. In 2020, three generations of Benchwicks had platters of cookies displayed on the enormous cookie table: Rachelle Benchwick, her son Ryan, daughters Carissa and Stephanie, and Ryan Benchwick's daughter, Sage, who baked these cookies and was awarded the title of 2020 Youngest Baker.

INGREDIENTS

½ cup Life Savers or Jolly Ranchers
¾ cup butter (1 and half sticks) softened
¼ cup sugar
1 teaspoon vanilla
2 cups flour
pinch of salt

Optional: food coloring for the dough.

PREPARATION

Unwrap and separate the candies by color (Life Savers or Jolly Ranchers) then place in separate small resealable bags. Crush into bits using a meat mallet; set aside.

Cream the butter and sugar until fluffy; add vanilla. If you would like to create a colored dough, add food coloring now; stir until completely blended. Add flour and salt, mix by hand until a dough is formed. Wrap dough in plastic wrap and chill for 30 minutes.

On a lightly floured surface, roll out dough ½-inch thick. Use any shaped cookie cutters desired, but you will need the cutters in two sizes: one for the cookie and one smaller to cut out the center "window" where the crushed hard candy will go to make the "glass." (Sage used heart-shape cookie cutters and the cookies were dyed in a variety of colors.)

Cut as many of the cookies as you can from the rolled-out dough; place these on an ungreased sheet covered with parchment paper. Using the smaller cookie cutter, cut out the inside shape, carefully peel away the cut piece of dough. You can bake these as mini cookies, without the candy, or set aside and re-use this dough.

Bake cookies at 350 degrees for 5 minutes. Remove from the oven and using a demitasse spoon carefully fill the hole in the middle of each cookie with the crushed candy, about ⅔ of the way full. (If you overfill it, the candy will bleed out on top of the dough.) Return to the oven and bake for about 7–10 more minutes, until cookies are golden brown. Do not transfer cookies yet! Allow the cookies to rest on the cookie sheet so that the liquified candy in the center of each cookie can cool and harden. Once candy has hardened, transfer cookies to a wire rack to cool completely.

Sugar Cookies

Scotia Naomi Cisler McKnight and Mary Potts

My Grandmother McKnight had five children: Aunt Ruth, Uncle Cloyce (we called him Uncle Cotton), Uncle Ed, Dave (my Dad), and Uncle Dick (Uncle Tiger). My Aunt Norma (Uncle Dick's widow) copied her Sugar Cookie recipe and the following story onto writing paper and gave all of the nieces and granddaughters a copy in 2013. "Grandma McKnight told me this recipe came with the first Hamilton Beach electric mixer that was bought for her by her sons Ed and Dave. Everyone else thought it was an old family recipe!" She was a great cook, fabulous cookie baker, and well loved. My daughter's wedding in September 2016 was the last family wedding she baked for and she baked fifty dozen cookies! She passed away just a few months later in December.

This is one of the easiest and speediest cookie recipes in this cookbook. No need to chill or roll out the dough, just drop it directly onto the cookie sheet. Perfect for weddings but also a quick sweet treat!

INGREDIENTS

½ cup margarine or butter (1 stick) softened
⅔ cup sugar
1 egg
1 tablespoon milk
1 teaspoon vanilla
1 ½ cups flour
½ teaspoon salt
1 teaspoon baking powder

PREPARATION

Preheat the oven to 375 degrees F.

Mix together the first five ingredients; add the flour, salt, and baking powder until fully combined. Drop dough by the heaping teaspoonful onto an ungreased cookie sheet. Optional: sprinkle tops with white sugar or other decorations before baking. Bake for 10-12 minutes. Transfer to a rack to cool.

Taralli

Rachael Barbour

My Grandmother Elisa came to Akron from Triggianno, a small town in Puglia, Italy. We grew up eating these sweet Taralli at Christmastime. If you do a quick search on Taralli, you will find that they are a ring-shaped cracker, delicious and savory. I don't know if these sweet Taralli are common, or just something Grandma Elisa made up—but for our family, it's not Christmas if there aren't Taralli. The recipe was transcribed by my Aunt Dorinda, watching my grandmother make the cookies.

These Taralli cookies were served as part of the cookie table for the 2015 wedding of Rachael's son Samuel Barbour and daughter-in-law Molly Breslin.

INGREDIENTS
COOKIES

2 cups all-purpose flour
2 cups whole wheat flour
5 teaspoons baking powder
1 teaspoon baking soda
1 cup neutral oil or 1 cup butter. softened
1 cup sugar
4 eggs
grated rind of 2-4 lemons
juice of one lemon

FROSTING

juice of 1 lemon
1 egg white
powdered sugar
nonpareil sprinkles

COOKIES

Preheat the oven to 350 degrees F.

Combine the flour, baking powder, and baking soda; set aside. Combine oil or butter, sugar, lemon juice, and lemon rind. Beat eggs into the sugar/oil mixture. Add dry mixture to the wet mixture and form a soft dough. If the dough is too sticky, you can add a bit more flour.

On a flat, floured surface, take some of the dough and roll out into a strand about ¼-inch thick. Cut into lengths of about 4 inches and tie into a loose knot. Place on a greased cookie sheet. Repeat. (An alternative shape is to twist together two strands and cut into lengths of about 3 or 4 inches.)

Bake for 10–12 minutes, or until a light golden brown. Place on a cooling rack (over a piece of newspaper). Immediately brush cookies with the frosting and decorate with a pinch of nonpareil sprinkles. The newspaper underneath will make cleanup a lot easier.

FROSTING

Place egg white and lemon juice in a mixing bowl. Add 1 cup of powdered sugar and mix until smooth. Continue adding powdered sugar and mixing until the frosting is opaque white but pours easily. This usually makes enough frosting for two batches of Taralli.

Welsh Cookies
(also known as Welsh Miner Cakes)

Judy Rohrbaugh

This recipe comes from Judy's husband's Grandmother Evans, who came to the U.S. from Wales in the late 1800s. It is a unique "cookie" in that it is cooked on an ungreased griddle on the stove, rather than baked in an oven. The texture has been compared to a cross between a scone, a pancake, and a cookie. The Welsh Baker blog (welshbaker.com) says that these cakes were just durable enough and the right size for a Welsh miner to slip into a coat pocket before heading off to work, and it was a way to enjoy a simple but sweet treat in the middle of an otherwise dreary work shift, down in the mines. It wasn't just the miners who enjoyed them: all across Wales they were a popular offering at afternoon teas and packed in children's lunches, and eventually the recipe was carried to America with Welsh immigrants who settled here.

INGREDIENTS

3 cups self-rising flour
1 ½ cups sugar
2 sticks of margarine or unsalted butter
2 eggs
1/2 cup currants or raisins (if using raisins, chop into smaller bits)
1/4 cup milk
2 teaspoons nutmeg
pinch of salt
granulated sugar (for sprinkling on top of finished cookies)

PREPARATION

In one bowl, mix the flour and sugar. Cut two sticks of cold margarine or butter into small pieces, then cut them into the flour/sugar mixture, blending them with your fingertips until the mixture resembles sand in texture. In a separate bowl, beat eggs, then add milk, nutmeg, pinch of salt, and currants or chopped raisins. Pour the milk and egg mixture into the flour mixture, and blend them with your hands until the dough resembles bread dough. Turn this out onto a well-floured surface and mix the last shaggy bits of dough together to form a ball. Split this ball in two, and take one section and roll it out to ¼-inch thick. Use a cookie cutter or biscuit cutter or glass to cut the dough into rounds between 2–3 inches in diameter.

On your stove top, heat a griddle to a medium to medium-low heat (an ungreased griddle works best) and place six cookies at a time to cook. Flip them after 2-4 minutes, or when they are golden brown and firm enough to flip. They will resemble little pancakes, or small round scones. When both sides are golden brown, lift them with a spatula to cool on a wire rack. When cool, sprinkle with granulated sugar.

Yola's Butter Balls

Marie McNulty

These recipes are scaled for exactly the kinds of quantities you'd need for bringing a large tray of cookies to a cookie table. All three recipes that I submitted have been in our family for sixty to seventy years. This Butter Ball recipe won me the Judges Award in 2014 at the Cookie Table and Cocktails event at the Tyler History Center in Youngstown, Ohio.

Marie notes that they should be small, no larger than 1 inch in diameter—just the size to pop in your mouth! Also, this is a triple recipe. If you want to scale it back, it can easily be cut by one third to make a single batch.

INGREDIENTS

6 sticks of butter
¾ cup powdered sugar
6 tablespoons milk
3 teaspoons vanilla
6 cups flour
6 cups finely ground nuts

PREPARATION

Preheat the oven to 350 degrees F.

Cream the butter; add powdered sugar, milk, and vanilla.

Add flour and nuts. Dough will be firm after mixing.

Roll into 1-inch balls and place on an ungreased cookie sheet.

Bake for about 20 minutes.

Cool completely and roll in powdered sugar.

Makes about 10 dozen cookies.

Yola's Chocolate Cookies

Marie McNulty

This is an old Italian recipe handed down from my mother, Yolanda "Viola" McNulty. It makes a TON of cookies. Mom usually made these cookies only at Christmastime or for special occasions. This recipe is one of our most cherished and favorite recipes from our mom.

INGREDIENTS

6 eggs
2 ½ cups sugar
1 pound Crisco
8 ounces honey
8 ounces Karo syrup
1 8-ounce can unsweetened cocoa powder
2 tablespoons vanilla
¼ teaspoon salt
¼ teaspoon cinnamon
6 ounces evaporated milk (half of a 12-ounce can)
¾ cup water
juice of 2 lemons + zest from grated rind
juice of 1 orange + zest from grated rind
½ pound finely chopped nuts
8 teaspoons baking powder
5 pounds flour

Preparation

Preheat the oven to 350 degrees F.

In a very large bowl, beat eggs. Add sugar, Crisco, honey, Karo syrup, cocoa, vanilla, salt, cinnamon, evaporated milk, and water. Mix well. Add the juice and grated rind of the lemons and orange. Stir to combine. Add chopped nuts and baking powder.

Add flour gradually until a stiff dough is formed. Use your best judgment.

Turn out onto a floured board and knead dough until the flour is incorporated. It should be shiny and firm.

Cut off a piece of dough and roll into a 1-inch by 12-inch strand, like a long chocolate snake. Cut on the diagonal to make cookies, about 2 inches each. They should be chubby, slightly rectangular pieces.

Place cookies on a lightly greased cookie sheet and bake for about 12-15 minutes. Transfer to cooling racks and let cool thoroughly.

Suggestion: make a thin icing of powdered sugar, water, and a little lemon juice. Mix it together and drizzle it on the cookies as they are cooling on racks. Be sure to use plenty of newspaper under the cookies to catch the icing as they dry.

Makes about 24 dozen cookies.

Are There Rules for Setting Up a Cookie Table?

There is only one rule: they should all be delicious. Other than that, there is no Cookie Table Rule Book that folks refer to. No cookie table police will show up at your celebration and give you a ticket if you aren't serving Pizzelles or Lady Locks. But there are a lot of common elements, most of which come down to tradition, preference, and practicality. Someone recently said in a food forum that you should never have chocolate chip cookies at a cookie table. It didn't say why and one could argue that they aren't considered fancy enough, but molasses and peanut butter cookies could fall into the same unfussy category and they are often found on cookie tables. So if a member of the wedding party absolutely loves chocolate chip cookies and someone on the baking team has a tried and true recipe, then by all means, serve them. We have included a recipe in this cookbook for Irish Soda Bread (it has a good backstory, related to the perception of cookie table rules) so we're obviously not afraid of bucking the convention a bit.

There are certain practical aspects of setting up a cookie table. People are often mindful to have cookies in a variety of colors, flavors, shapes, and textures. (Although a completely monochromatic cookie table would be both dramatic and different.) Cookies should not be too gooey or hard to handle. If they are a bit decadent, like a Baklava, or prone to melting, like a small truffle, it is wise to serve those in small paper cups. And size does matter—you're better off providing bite-sized cookies than those the size of your palm. This is a win-win for those that are baking them and those that are planning on eating a small plateful of them.

Speaking of those that are doing the baking; people often ask if it's OK to farm out some of the cookies to a professional baker or caterer, rather than having your entire family bake every single cookie. Being able to claim that *all* of the cookies on the cookie table were made by family and friends continues to be a very strong point of pride. But others have mentioned hiring a professional to make a custom cookie just for the occasion, especially those that make the intricately hand-decorated cookies, say in the likeness of the wedding couple or a college mascot. In terms of set up, many cookie tables utilize cake stands, platforms, or tiered trays that allow for different heights of cookie platters. This is both pleasing to the eye and allows you to fit in more plates of cookies.

How many cookies you might ask? That is totally dependent upon you and your cookie baking crew. It is not unheard of for people to start baking in earnest months before the big celebration and freezing the cookies, and there's a certain amount of bragging rights that go along with serving very large quantities of cookies. But ultimately, you'll make as many cookies as makes sense. Do remember that the tradition assumes that people will take a few cookies home. It seems to be a more recent component, but people now will put out little boxes or bags so that guests can take some cookies home, and often encourage them to do so with a little sign on the table. You still might catch your Aunt Nancy wrapping a few cookies in a cocktail napkin and tucking them into her purse, because that's been the way to go for as long as anyone can remember.

Acknowledgments

Just as a wondrous cookie table is by its very nature a group effort, this cookbook would not have been possible without all the people who gave it their time and skills. Sincere thanks to all of the recipe contributors. It was an absolute delight to work with each of you and share so many baking stories and memories in the process.

A special thanks to Linda Kostko with the Mahoning Valley Historical Society, Jacqueline Marino at Kent State University, and Linda Sproul with the Youngstown Cookie Table Facebook group, for helping me connect with many of the keepers of the cookie recipes.

Thank you to Eiren Caffall, Sarah Steedman, and Rachel Weber for your generosity with recipe testing, editing, and feedback.

I am especially grateful to Martha Bayne and Belt Publishing for trusting me with this project. Martha is a superb editor who kept me moving along, during a pandemic no less, with grace, humor, and impeccable word-crafting skills. Thanks as well go to Belt Publishing's Anne Trubek for her stewardship of Rust Belt voices and communities, to David Wilson for the adorable cover design, and to Meredith Pangrace, who meticulously designed the interior.

And I thank my husband Ted for his unwavering enthusiasm, and my sons Sam and Ben for coming into the kitchen, putting on aprons, and helping me bake (and eat) many of the cookies in this book. Grandma Sally and Pop-Pops would be so tickled by all of this.

About the Author

Bonnie Tawse is a writer and home baker committed to exploring the connections between food, community, and culture. She has co-hosted a Nordic Dinner series, is a former Atlas Obscura Field Agent, and helped establish children's organic gardens in parks all over Chicago. Her writing has appeared in *TimeOut Chicago Kids*, *Chicago Parent*, and for institutions such as the Cultural Landscapes Foundation and the Lurie Garden. She holds an M.A. in Creative Writing from CU Boulder, and her fiction has been published in *ChickLit 2*, *Asylum Arts Annual*, and *Sniper Logic*. She lives in Chicago with her husband and two sons and recently spent a year visiting and celebrating 52 Bakeries in 52 Weeks.